W9-ACW-145

Ian K. Macgillivray, PhD

Gay-Straight Alliances
A Handbook for Students, Educators, and Parents

Pre-publication
REVIEWS,
COMMENTARIES,
EVALUATIONS . . .

"**M**ore and more youth are taking on leadership roles in transforming the culture and climate of schools across the nation, particularly regarding the pervasive bias that exists against lesbian, gay, bisexual, and transgender people. Macgillivray's important new handbook could not have come at a better time. Drawing broadly on empirical and legal research, as well as personal experience, *Gay-Straight Alliances* offers vital and helpful information, resources, and advice for students, educators, parents, and leaders in creating and supporting GSAs."

Kevin K. Kumashiro, PhD
Associate Professor,
College of Education,
University of Illinois-Chicago;
Director, Center for Anti-Oppressive Education

"**W**hat a refreshing look at the facts and issues surrounding gay-straight alliances. Dr. Macgillivray provides information from the point of view of what GLBT youth can provide schools to upgrade their safety level, improve their understanding of GLBT issues, and advocate for the rights of all students, not from the point of view of 'victims' but from the knowledge that many students–GLBTQ and their allies–have a lot to offer the diverse populations of their schools. The information and resources provided here cover anything anyone from the students themselves to the school administrators and school boards would need to have a GSA work and thrive in their school community. Our PFLAG parents and allies will find it a valuable addition to their safe schools work in rural, urban, and suburban areas alike."

Judy Hoff, MS/Ed
Senior Coordinator,
Safe Schools,
PFLAG National

Gay-Straight Alliances
A Handbook for Students, Educators, and Parents

HARRINGTON PARK PRESS®
Haworth Series on GLBT Youth & Adolescence
James T. Sears
Editor

Gay-Straight Alliances: A Handbook for Students, Educators, and Parents by Ian K. Macgillivray

Titles of Related Interest

Coming Out of the Classroom Closet: Gay and Lesbian Students, Teachers, and Curricula edited by Karen M. Harbeck

Gay and Lesbian Youth edited by Gilbert Herdt

Gay, Lesbian, and Transgender Issues in Education: Programs, Policies, and Practices edited by James T. Sears

Handbook of LGBT Issues in Community Mental Health edited by Ronald E. Hellman and Jack Drescher

Helping Gay and Lesbian Youth: New Policies, New Programs, New Practice edited by Teresa DeCrescenzo

Homosexuality and the Family edited by Frederick W. Bozett

How Homophobia Hurts Children: Nurturing Diversity at Home, at School, and in the Community by Jean M. Baker

In Your Face: Stories from the Lives of Queer Youth edited by Mary L. Gray

Male Bodies, Women's Souls: Personal Narratives of Thailand's Transgendered Youth by LeeRay M. Costa and Andrew J. Matzner

Queer Kids: The Challenges and Promise for Lesbian, Gay, and Bisexual Youth by Robert E. Owens Jr.

Queering Teen Culture: All-American Boys and Same-Sex Desire in Film and Television by Jeffrey P. Dennis

School Experiences of Gay and Lesbian Youth: The Invisible Minority edited by Mary B. Harris

Social Services with Transgendered Youth edited by Gerald P. Mallon

Gay-Straight Alliances
A Handbook for Students, Educators, and Parents

Ian K. Macgillivray, PhD

HPP

Harrington Park Press®
The Trade Division of The Haworth Press, Inc.
New York • London

For more information on this book or to order, visit
http://www.haworthpress.com/store/product.asp?sku=5921

or call 1-800-HAWORTH (800-429-6784) in the United States and Canada
or (607) 722-5857 outside the United States and Canada
or contact orders@HaworthPress.com

Published by

Harrington Park Press®, the trade division of The Haworth Press, Inc., 10 Alice Street, Binghamton, NY 13904-1580.

PUBLISHER'S NOTE
The development, preparation, and publication of this work has been undertaken with great care. However, the Publisher, employees, editors, and agents of The Haworth Press are not responsible for any errors contained herein or for consequences that may ensue from use of materials or information contained in this work. The Haworth Press is committed to the dissemination of ideas and information according to the highest standards of intellectual freedom and the free exchange of ideas. Statements made and opinions expressed in this publication do not necessarily reflect the views of the Publisher, Directors, management, or staff of The Haworth Press, Inc., or an endorsement by them.

Cover design by Jennifer M. Gaska.

Library of Congress Cataloging-in-Publication Data

Macgillivray, Ian K., 1967-
    Gay-straight alliances : a handbook for students, educators, and parents / Ian K. Macgillivray.
        p. cm.
    Includes bibliographical references and index.
    ISBN: 978-1-56023-684-9 (hard : alk. paper)
    ISBN: 978-1-56023-685-6 (soft : alk. paper)
    1. Gay high school students—Societies, etc.—Handbooks, manuals, etc. 2. Sexual minority students—Societies, etc.—Handbooks, manuals, etc. 3. High school environment—Handbooks, manuals, etc. 4. School management and organization—Handbooks, manuals, etc. 5. Gay rights—Handbooks, manuals, etc. I. Title.

LC2574.5.M33 2007
373.1826'64—dc22

                                                                                    2006036545

This book is dedicated to all the students
who have the courage to start gay-straight alliances
and to the educators and parents who support them.

ABOUT THE AUTHOR

Ian K. Macgillivray, PhD, is Assistant Professor of Foundations of Education at James Madison University in Virginia, and the author of *Sexual Orientation and School Policy: A Practical Guide for Teachers, Administrators, and Community Activists.* He is a former middle and high school teacher and continues his work with students, school districts, and preservice teachers on issues of lesbian, gay, bisexual, and transgender student rights. For more information or to contact the author, please visit www.ianmacgillivray .com.

CONTENTS

Foreword

A few months ago, I attended a "Love Won Out" conference brought to Boston (and elsewhere in the United States) by Focus on the Family, its parent organization. Led by some people claiming to have overcome their own homosexuality, the goal of this conference was to prove that gays and lesbians can become heterosexual by means of Christian faith and psychological deprogramming. Presenters condemned the inducements to homosexual sin that abound in contemporary culture—among them, changing sex roles, liberal media, and the gay agenda.

One aspect of gay activism they portrayed as especially sinister is the increasing number of gay-straight alliances (GSAs) in the schools. A college education professor led the session "Why Is What They're Teaching So Dangerous?" He warned that, under the guise of "safety," homosexual radicals were subverting the will of the majority of parents who don't want their children to be exposed to gay propaganda. The radicals have a clever strategy, he admitted—who could be against safe schools?

As I read Ian K. Macgillivray's levelheaded and practical handbook, I am struck by its moderation and reasonableness. Who could oppose his recommendations and guidelines? Then I recall the "Love Won Out" attendees, sighing apprehensively at the warnings about gay activists plotting in the schools.

So when Macgillivray writes, "Demonstrating that GSAs are one way to enhance school safety for students, based on their real or perceived sexual orientation and gender identity, may help to build understanding with the opposition" (p. 66), the tactic is exactly what opponents have been admonished to be ready for.

Gay-Straight Alliances: A Handbook for Students, Educators, and Parents
© 2007 by The Haworth Press, Inc. All rights reserved.
doi:10.1300/5921_a

Thankfully, Macgillivray doesn't end there; he carefully parses the opposition and offers excellent advice on how to deal with them respectfully.

Macgillivray's respect for his opponents does not, however, lead him to abandon the notion that public education must be guided by more than parents' wishes. "Public education is about the free and open exchange of ideas" (p. 78). Moreover, we cannot forget that for some, the free exchange of competing ideas—especially about right and wrong—is not a welcome educational project: "If the child of religious fundamentalist parents comes to believe 'It's okay to be gay,' it's because the child arrived at that conclusion on his or her own, not because he or she was coerced into that belief. This is the very possibility, however, that religious fundamentalist parents want to prevent" (p. 62).

Cognitive restraints imposed at home may be jostled loose by inquiry, discussion, and student disputation. The dissonance they experience can lead students to question their home, community, and church values. Liberals see this process as growth; the right see it as heresy.

Even when the GSA serves merely as a safe place for lesbian, gay, bisexual, and transgender (LGBT) youth, it may still be a gall to conservatives. As Macgillivray observes, GSAs are "a safe place for students to get the support they sometimes cannot get at home" (p. 11). Precisely: opponents do not want schools to undermine antigay parents by "abetting" their gay children or by giving the impression that schools should do so.

Although Macgillivray writes, "parents who oppose GSAs may be able to prohibit their child from attending one, but they do not have the right to prevent other peoples' children from attending one" (p. 66), the right of parents to keep their own children from joining GSAs ("opt-in" requirements) is not legally established. However, in Georgia, parental "opt-in" requirements are now legal in specific instances. Georgia schools are now required to inform parents or guardians of the available extracurricular activities the school offers, with the option to "opt-out" their child from particular clubs by signing a form. If students form a club after parents are notified of available clubs, then "opt-in" forms must be signed by parents (Bagby, 2006). Meanwhile, a California judge has ruled that a student who sued her school for informing her parents that she is gay, "sufficiently alleged a legally protected privacy interest in information about her sexual orientation" (Lewin, 2005). GSA membership may yet prove to be a matter of private choice for students.

Of course, GSAs are not "sex clubs," but they can facilitate access to information about sex, safer sex, HIV/STD prevention, and so on. In schools lacking comprehensive LGBT-inclusive health education, the GSA can be a literal lifeline for students who are sexually active.

Nor can we say often enough that GSAs are not just for LGBT students. As Macgillivray observes, "many teens who are involved in GSAs identify as heterosexual. Their reasons for joining a GSA might be to show support for their LGBT friends, practice civil involvement in a worthy cause, or just to be with their friends who are involved in one" (p. 71). My observation as a former GSA advisor is that GSAs attract student nonconformists in general, perhaps because they seek an escape from peer pressure and conventional judgment, whatever their particular eccentricities.

With its gay, straight, bisexual, queer, or unaffiliated membership, GSAs do make a political statement, explicit or implied. Although, they do not represent an "official endorsement of homosexuality" (p. 11) on the part of school officials and they are not about "forcing anybody to agree, 'it's okay to be gay'" (p. 11), their existence and activities do attest that "gay is good"—to borrow a phrase from the previous century.

Macgillivray freely admits the utility of antigay abuse stories to move school boards to approve programs for LGBT youth. Yet, he understands that GSAs must help students "get over their victimization" (p. 29). He advocates a politics of self-empowerment over self-pity and mutual complaint. Such advocacy goes directly to the nexus of the personal and the political. "School was perceived to be no longer a place to be avoided, but as a place to confront the heterosexism and homophobia . . . They became empowered personally and collectively by working toward a common goal (challenging the system in which they previously believed they could not have an impact)" (Garcia-Alonso 2004, p. 77).

Macgillivray cites Pat Griffin's exhortation that tolerance is not enough: "[T]he GSA should help the school to become more socially just by addressing the ways in which the curriculum, policies, and practices of the school privilege heterosexuals and exclude LGBT students" (p. 33). Those are patriarchy-dismantling words.

Yet, along with the political stance that could sweep a GSA into controversy, this book also contains good advice to keep it from foundering. For example, because GSAs invariably whither and thrive over the years, student members need encouragement, but not adult-imposed agendas; schools should avoid sponsoring "speech that analyzes the rightness or wrongness of various religions" (p. 53); and students need protection against direct harassment, but broad speech codes discourage a necessary expression of ideas in schools.

These are the kinds of sound suggestions that make this manual so valuable.

Arthur Lipkin, EdD
Cambridge, MA

Preface

Across the nation, lesbian, gay, bisexual, and transgender (LGBT) students are proclaiming their identities and demanding equal treatment from their schools. Religious fundamentalist parents, on the other hand, are organizing themselves in opposition to what they perceive as a "gay agenda" to "promote homosexuality" to America's youth. Schools are caught in the middle of this debate. Legislative bodies and courts are in the midst of defining how this debate will play out legally.

I wrote this book to help students, educators, and parents wade through the social, legal, and procedural issues that accompany the establishment of gay-straight alliances (GSAs) in their schools. As a high school teacher, I helped a group of my students start a GSA at our school. Now, as a university professor, I continue to work with high school students who are starting GSAs in their own schools, as well as the teachers who advise them. In my first book, *Sexual Orientation and School Policy: A Practical Guide for Teachers, Administrators, and Community Activists,* I gave one community's story of how a safe schools coalition worked with a group of religious fundamentalist parents to make their schools safer for all students. Recently, in my own community, the school board and high school administrators were caught unawares between opposing sides over a new GSA at the high school. All of these experiences helped me realize the need for a book on GSAs.

I have organized the chapters to enable quick and easy access to information. Some chapters will be of more interest to some read-

Gay-Straight Alliances: A Handbook for Students, Educators, and Parents
© 2007 by The Haworth Press, Inc. All rights reserved.
doi:10.1300/5921_b *xiii*

ers than others will. Although each chapter can stand alone, reading the entire book will provide a "big picture" of all the issues surrounding GSAs. Either way, the book is meant to be used as a handy reference guide. If you know of a resource that is not listed in this book or feel I have overlooked something, I would enjoy hearing from you so I can include that information in future editions. Finally, nothing I say in this book is meant to provide legal advice. If you have specific legal questions, you should seek the services of a qualified, licensed attorney. I hope you will find this book useful. Enjoy and good luck!

Acknowledgments

Not everyone can say they love their work, so I count myself fortunate that I have my dream job. I wanted to write books and be a professor of education so I could prepare tomorrow's teachers to help their own students to work for social justice. I have learned that the hardest, yet most rewarding part of my job is the challenge posed to me by my students to evolve my own thinking. I am grateful to my students for that. I also want to thank my colleagues and friends in the College of Education at James Madison University, who have supported me and eased my transition back into life in academia and in the United States.

Y muchas gracias a mis amigos de el México, D. F.—Peggy Bayles, Ramon Garcia, Jesus Rechy, Carlos Pérez, Julia (en la bodega), Mish, Adelaida, Laura, Nadia, Vicente y Demaris. *Los extraño mucho a todos.*

This book would not be complete without the most gracious contributions of Dr. Brett Genny Beemyn of Transgender Law and Policy Institute; Chris Hampton of ACLU's Lesbian and Gay Rights Project; and Carolyn Laub, Founder and Executive Director of Gay-Straight Alliance Network. I would also like to extend many thanks and acknowledge the contributions of Dominique Johnson; Joshua Kletzkin and Joe Kosciw of GLSEN; Tracy Lederman; Lance McCready; Pat Griffin; Lisa Mottet; my series editor, James T. Sears; and the editors at Haworth Press.

What would I do without my friends? Steven Hopp and Lyle Jackson, Steve Fairchild and Bob Olmstead, Cheri Beverly, Sabrina Stahn and Jerry Kunkle, David L. Francis (this book was begun on

Gay-Straight Alliances: A Handbook for Students, Educators, and Parents
© 2007 by The Haworth Press, Inc. All rights reserved.
doi:10.1300/5921_c   *xv*

his computer, Christmas 2004), Robert Davis, Daryl J. Walker, Thomas Lavenir, Fabricio Solorzano, James Hathaway and Sean Pugh, and Aaron Bunch and Curtis Sheets—you guys keep me going.

Mom, Dad, Magi, Aaron, Riley, and Phoebe—you are my rock.

Chapter 1

What Is a Gay-Straight Alliance?

A gay-straight alliance (GSA) is a student club that provides a safe place for students to discuss issues that are important to them, to meet others with similar interests, and to get support from one another and from caring adults. GSAs have been around since the late 1980s. The very first GSA was formed in 1988 by a group of students at a high school in Massachusetts, advised by Kevin Jennings, Executive Director of the Gay, Lesbian, Straight Education Network (GLSEN), who was then a history teacher. Since then, GSAs have spread across the country and around the world. There are now more than 3000 GSAs in all fifty states in the United States and the numbers increase almost every day (GLSEN, 2005).

GSAs are open to all students and serve an especially important role for lesbian, gay, bisexual, and transgender (LGBT) students, children of LGBT parents, and straight student allies. Like any other student club, GSAs are started by students, for students. According to the 1984 Federal Equal Access Act, people from the community cannot initiate or regularly attend student clubs in public schools. Although teachers and other school personnel are permitted to supervise student clubs, the agendas are set by the students and the meetings are student-led.

GSAs usually meet during lunch or after school and like any student club, may not interfere with regular class time. The 1984

Gay-Straight Alliances: A Handbook for Students, Educators, and Parents
© 2007 by The Haworth Press, Inc. All rights reserved.
doi:10.1300/5921_01

Federal Equal Access Act requires that GSAs be treated like any other school club, which includes equal access to funding, school newspapers, yearbook photos, meeting space, bulletin boards, and the public address system. The law mandates that as long as a school allows one student club to meet on school grounds, it must allow the same for all other student clubs (see Chapter 4 for provisions and exceptions to this rule). Students in GSAs engage in similar activities as other clubs, which may include organizing fund-raisers and other social events, peer education and support, community service, and political activism. Belonging to a GSA, or any other student club for that matter, provides students with opportunities to associate with others who have similar interests and to extend their educational experiences beyond the classroom.

GSAs are not without their detractors, however. Religious fundamentalist parents are usually the first to object when a school in their community forms a GSA. Their main concern is that the school will teach their children values with which they disagree. These parents believe that schools endorse homosexuality when they allow GSAs to form and that it sends the message "It's okay to be gay." Religious fundamentalist parents do not want their children getting this message in school. They also believe that being gay entails only one thing—sex. Thus, they are left to conclude that GSAs promote sex, which is why they sometimes refer to GSAs as "sex clubs." What they do not understand, however, is that being gay entails much more than sex, just as being straight entails more than sex.

SEXUAL ORIENTATION

Everybody has a sexual orientation. It encompasses to whom one is attracted, both sexually and romantically. LGBT is the acronym most often used to refer to people who are not heterosexual and/or not gender typical—that is, people who bend the rules of gender. It's easier to say "LGBT" than it is "lesbian, gay, bisexual, and transgender." Many people add Q to the acronym—as in LGBTQ—and Q stands for "queer." Whereas queer was once a dirty word, it has since been reclaimed by some people who proudly label themselves as queer. Some see it as a political statement, and others believe the term includes all people who are not hetero-sexual, or who do not fit into traditional gender role stereotypes.

When discussing sexual orientation, it is important to make the distinction between *identity* and *behavior*. For instance, one sexual experience with a person of the same sex does not make one gay or bisexual. Also, a celibate person can identify as gay or straight. That is, one's identity as gay or straight is not defined solely by who they have sex with. More important, it includes *identification* and *association* with others who claim the same sexual orientation. The important point is that one can discuss sexual orientation and give examples of what makes a person straight, gay, or bisexual without mentioning sex.

Straight people do and say things all the time, without even re-alizing that it identifies them as heterosexual. For instance, they wear wedding bands, display pictures of their spouse and children on their desks, they elect a prom king and queen (as opposed to two kings or two queens), and they freely discuss their boyfriends, girlfriends, and spouses with others. Straight peoples' identifica-tion as "straight," and their association with other heterosexuals, does not revolve around sex. It's the same for gay, lesbian, and bisexual people too.

Though labels such as "gay," "straight," and "LGBT" are popu-larly used, they are not reflective of the fluidity of human sexual-ity. Nowadays, many adolescents with same-sex attractions do not use "gay" as their primary identifier because they place more im-portance on other aspects of themselves, for instance, their race or ethnicity, religion, or athletic or musical ability (Savin-Williams, 2005). Adolescents with same-sex attractions have the same con-cerns, worries, hopes, and dreams as heterosexual adolescents. Most of them are happy and well-adjusted, and worry more about zits than to whom they're attracted. The point is, for most adolescents, their sexual orientations and gender identities are not a big deal, and we should respect their rights by not forcing them to choose a label.

GENDER IDENTITY

Gender identity and sexual orientation are two separate issues, but transgender people and LGB people share many of the same concerns. Gender identity is a person's identification as male, female, both, neither, or somewhere in between. Transgender (the T in LGBT) includes a broad spectrum of people, from those who privately do not identify as their birth sex but do nothing about it, to those who cross-dress sometimes or always, to those who change their body to match their identity with hormone therapy and sex-reassignment surgery. A person's gender identity is independent of their sexual orientation. For example, a person who is anatomically female but who identifies as male may be sexually and romantically attracted to either or both males and females.

Intersex

Very recently, intersex people have begun to speak up and align themselves with LGBT people, again because they share some of the same concerns and oppressions. Intersex refers to people who were born with a genetic, hormonal, or physical anatomy that is not regarded as completely male or female. Intersex people were previously and sometimes incorrectly referred to as hermaphrodites. The Web site of the Intersex Society of North America (www .isna.org) explains, "Intersexuality constitutes a range of anatomical conditions in which an individual's anatomy mixes key masculine anatomy with key feminine anatomy." Examples of being intersex include: not having the standard complement of chromosomes that genetically make one a male or female (1 in 1,666 births); various syndromes that affect the body's production of or reaction to hormones, such as androgen insensitivity syndrome (1 in 13,000 births); and reproductive organs and genitals that are not fully formed as male or female (1 or 2 in 1,000 births receive some type of surgery to "normalize" the appearance of the genitals) (ISNA, 2005). We often don't hear of intersex people because of the stigma that surrounds being intersex. Intersex people often don't know they are intersex, and if they do, usually prefer to keep that information private.

ARE GSAs SEX CLUBS?

Many religious fundamentalist parents do not want students to have information on sexual orientation and gender identity because it questions traditional gender roles for men and women and their belief that everybody is or should be heterosexual. All people are not heterosexual, however, and schools must deal with this reality. All students, and especially students who are LGBT, need accurate information about sexual orientation and gender identity to help them grow and develop into healthy and well-adjusted adults. To say that GSAs are all about sex misses the point that students have different sexual orientations and gender identities and naturally seek out others like themselves for social activities. Although a Bible club may promote the idea that all people should be heterosexual, it does not promote the idea that students should therefore run out and have heterosexual sex. Likewise, although a GSA may promote the idea that "It's okay to be gay," it does not promote that students should engage in gay sex. Being straight or being gay entails much more than sex.

WHY DO STUDENTS START
GAY-STRAIGHT ALLIANCES?

Students start GSAs for a variety of reasons, but usually their purposes are social, educational, political, service to the community, or the need for support. LGBT students, students who are perceived to be LGBT (because of who they're friends with, how they dress, their mannerisms, and so on), and students with LGBT parents are frequently the targets of bullying and ridicule by other students. Coping with this abuse from one's peers is different for LGBT students because they most often cannot expect support from their families, as opposed to kids who are teased for being geeks, overweight, or poor. Many LGBT students are afraid to tell their parents they are or might be LGBT for the fear of upsetting their parents, at best, or getting thrown out of their homes, at worst. That leaves school as the most frequent place where LGBT students can turn for support. LGBT students, and their allies, need safe spaces in which to support one another and get guidance from caring and supportive adults (such as teachers and counselors). Without support or safe social outlets, the isolation and bullying that some LGBT students experience in America's schools may lead to drug and alcohol abuse, low academic achievement, depression, and suicide (Human Rights Watch, 2001). In providing a balanced perspective of the lives of youth with same-sex attraction and nontraditional gender identities, however, it is important to note that the majority of them are happy, well-adjusted, and do not attempt suicide or engage in risk-taking behaviors (Savin-Williams, 2005).

Youth Voices

Closeted LGBT youths feel like they have to hide themselves because their high school will look down upon them and insult them. They have to worry about their safety and try to act as a straight kid. This causes low self-esteem and this can be depressing. I know this because I have been there. After I came out, though, I had more challenges, which were my parents' reactions. In the beginning, we cried and fought, and getting past that whole acceptance part was hard . . . My parents wanted me to stay closeted throughout high school, which I also didn't want to do. I chose to tell my friends. That's all who know but granted, a lot of people know. When I am at work, I am so afraid that one of my friends will come in and will just say something that could imply I was gay and that would have my fellow workers know that I was gay. I don't want them to know. It's not their business. I think another challenge is meeting LGBT youth. I know, right now, what I am really missing is just a friend who has gone through what I have. My straight friends are great and supportive, but they don't really know. I can't go to them and tell them who I like and want to date and stuff. They would get a little weirded-out by that. We go through a lot of stuff alone.

—Gay male high school student (Sampson, 2000, p. 60)

HOW DO GAY-STRAIGHT ALLIANCES HELP ALL STUDENTS?

GSAs provide a safe space for students to develop their social skills, get support and information that is age-appropriate, and meet others with similar interests, which helps end the social and emotional isolation some LGBT teens experience. GSAs can also improve safety for all students by providing educational programs that decrease harassment and bullying. Furthermore, the opportunities for social and political activism that a GSA can provide help students to gain self-confidence and build character. There is a growing body of research that highlights the benefits of GSAs.

Youth Voices

I think the primary reason that LGBT kids seem to engage in more risky behavior is that we often feel alone. I personally have been so lucky that I attend a school with a great GSA. I have supportive teachers and wonderful gay adults I can talk with and friends who have been so amazing . . . believe me, I know how lucky I am to have all of this . . . I really don't know what I would have done if my friends hadn't supported me or if I was so nervous that I couldn't even tell my friends the truth or if I didn't have such great gay role models. I don't think I would feel so hopeful and excited about my life and be able to see firsthand how successful and happy gays and lesbians can be. We need to let other students who are so scared and angry at themselves for being gay, who might turn to drugs and unsafe sex to deal with their confusion, know that it is all right and that they will be fine and live happy lives. I think having positive role models is vital for any kids, but especially LGBT youth.

                          —Lesbian high school student (Sampson, 2000, p. 62)

Scientific Research

According to Paula Sampson (2000), a graduate student and faculty advisor of a GSA in Massachusetts, the 1997 Massachusetts Youth Risk Behavior Survey (MYRBS) data show that gay, lesbian, and bisexual students who endure social isolation or bullying at school are more likely to engage in risky behavior than are their heterosexual peers. Sampson used the MYRBS data to conduct her own research to determine if GSAs reduce levels of risk-taking behavior of gay, lesbian, and bisexual students. Sampson compared the results of the 1997 MYRBS with her own survey completed in five schools with GSAs in Massachusetts during the 1999-2000 school year. She used the same survey instrument used by MYRBS, selected forty-five questions from it (that related to risk-taking behaviors in the four survey areas of sexual behavior, violence, suicide, and drug and alcohol use), and added four questions to determine the participant's involvement in their school's GSA.

According to Sampson (2000), the students surveyed for her research "reported engaging in fewer risky behaviors in almost every category measured, than their gay and lesbian counterparts in the [previous] 1997 MYRBS study" (p. 73). The data indicate a correlation between involvement in a GSA and the students being the following:

- Less likely to have multiple sex partners
- Less likely to have used drugs or alcohol before sex

- Less likely to have had sex ever
- Less likely to carry a weapon
- Less likely to be in a fight at school
- Less likely to consider suicide
- Less likely to attempt suicide
- Less likely to have used alcohol or injected drugs (pp. 73-75)

Sampson (2000) concludes:

> Clearly, the challenges faced by gay and lesbian youth are formidable, but the results of this survey indicate that there may be hope for constructing effective school support systems . . . All [students surveyed] expressed the need for their GSAs to become visible and active agents for change in their own schools . . . while continuing to provide support on a personal level. The [GSAs] provide a place where students can relax and regroup their energy to face another day or another week at school. (p. 76)

Another study was conducted by the California Safe Schools Coalition and 4-H Center for Youth Development (2004). It reports the results of the "2003 Preventing School Harassment" survey administered to 634 middle and high school students in California, 46 percent of respondents identified as LGBT. The survey asked students about their perceptions of safety in their schools and their experiences with antigay and antitrans bullying and harassment. Students reported that they were more likely to feel safe, more likely to report safe school climates, and less likely to be harassed if their schools took any or all of these five steps:

1. Establish a policy that prohibits discrimination based on sexual orientation and gender identity.
2. Train teachers and staff to stop slurs and harassment.
3. Support the establishment of a GSA or similar student clubs.
4. Ensure that students know whom to approach for support and information related to sexual orientation and gender identity.

5. Introduce curriculum that includes LGBT people and information about sexual orientation and gender identity. (pp. 17-23)

Another study by Griffin, Lee, Waugh, and Beyer (2004) surveyed twenty-two high schools and found that GSAs provide many benefits to students. Among the benefits that the study reports are "help individual students work through identity issues and the accompanying stresses . . . members can meet with peers who share similar values . . . [and help LGBT students] overcome persistent isolation and victimization in school." Finally, the study reports that GSAs effectively help schools change individual behavior (such as antigay bullying), but the next step should be for GSAs to make "more substantial institutional changes" by becoming "part of a broad on-going effort to make schools safe and welcoming for all students, staff, and families" (p. 20).

Several other studies also report the benefits of GSAs. Lee, in Griffin et al. (2004), reports that "GSA membership had a positive impact on students' academic performance, enhanced their sense of physical safety in the school, increased their perceived ability to contribute to society, and contributed to a greater sense of belonging to the school community" (p. 9). Likewise, Doppler, in Griffin et al. (2004), reported that GSAs "replaced isolation with connection for GSA members, provided opportunities for positive risk-taking, and contributed to a new vision for school climate and culture" (p. 9). And Szalacha, in Griffin et al. (2004), reported that in schools with GSAs, students were "less likely to hear antigay slurs" (p. 9).

SUMMARY

Gay-straight alliances are:

- Student clubs started and run by students, for students
- Required under federal law to be treated like any other student club

- A safe place for students to get the support they sometimes cannot get at home
- A good way to end the social and emotional isolation endured by some LGBT students
- An effective way to educate the school community about equality and diversity
- Shown to decrease bullying, violence, and risky behaviors
- Often opposed by religious fundamentalists

Gay-straight alliances are not:

- Sex clubs
- An official endorsement of homosexuality
- Only for LGBT students
- Forcing anybody to agree, "It's okay to be gay"

WEB RESOURCES

Gay-Straight Alliance Network (GSA Network)
www.gsanetwork.org

Gay, Lesbian, Straight Education Network (GLSEN)
jumpstart@glsen.org
studentorganizing@glsen.org
www.glsen.org

Parents, Families, and Friends of Lesbians and Gays (PFLAG)
www.pflag.org

The Safe Schools Coalition
www.safeschoolscoalition.org/RG-gaystraightalliances.html

Chapter 2

For Students:
Starting a GSA in Your School

If your school allows other noncurricular clubs, such as a chess club or Young Life, then your school also must allow a gay-straight alliance (GSA). If you're unsure whether your district allows noncurricular clubs then ask a teacher, administrator, or school board member to get you a copy of the school board's policy on student clubs. You might also be able to find it yourself on your district's Web site, under "school board policy."

DO SOME BACKGROUND RESEARCH BEFORE YOU BEGIN

GSA Network

The GSA Network has tons of resources to help students start GSAs. Check them out at www.gsanetwork.org.

American Civil Liberties Union (ACLU)

The ACLU's Lesbian and Gay Rights Project is a great guide to the legal aspects of starting a GSA. Check them out at www.aclu.org/getequal/scho/alliance.html or e-mail getequal@aclu.org.

Gay, Lesbian, Straight Education Network (GLSEN)

GLSEN has free activity guides for GSAs on its Web site. Go to www.glsen.org, click on "Students" and then click on "Jump Start Your Student Club" under "Student Library." Or you can e-mail them for more information at jumpstart@glsen.org.

Gay-Straight Alliances: A Handbook for Students, Educators, and Parents
© 2007 by The Haworth Press, Inc. All rights reserved.
doi:10.1300/5921_02

Lambda Legal Defense and Education Fund

The Lambda Legal Defense and Education Fund has an online guide that explains students' rights. The title is *Out, Safe, & Respected: Your Rights at School* and it's available at www.lambdalegal.org/cgi-bin/ iowa/youthpsa/index.html?page=youth_index

HOW TO START A GSA
IN TEN NOT-SO-EASY STEPS

GSAs are usually started by a small group of students who follow a procedure similar to the following:

1. You must be absolutely certain you want to do this. This may put you in the spotlight.
2. Find a teacher or counselor whom you trust to be an advisor for the GSA.
3. Get the required form from the office for starting a new student club.
4. Make a list of objectives and goals.
5. Decide on a mission statement that reflects your objectives.
6. Decide if you will have a president, vice president, secretary, and treasurer, or alternative leadership, such as rotating facilitators or a steering committee, and choose a name for your club.
7. Prepare information on GSAs and the 1984 Equal Access Act for your principal.
8. Submit the New Student Club form and meet with the principal.
9. Be patient. It's not going to happen overnight.
10. Protect yourself if things get ugly.

Step One

Step number one is the most important when it comes to protecting your privacy and making sure you're ready to deal with any negative attention that may come your way. I counseled Kerry Pacer, a high school junior in White County, Georgia, who started the first GSA in her rural conservative area. She was really excited that the principal eventually approved the GSA, but as soon as the community found out about it, many residents started directing hateful comments at her and her family. The situation turned ugly really fast and caught her off guard. You have to think about the possibility of people in your community and school being very angry with you. They may say and do some really mean things and you need to protect yourself. If you have the support of your parent(s), that's great, but unfortunately, that's not realistic for every person. Hopefully, you will also have the support of some caring teachers, administrators, and friends in your school. Your community might also have a Safe Schools Coalition; an LGBT community center; or local chapters of Parents, Families, and Friends of Lesbians and Gays (PFLAG); or GLSEN. You can usually rely on them to help you get started too.

Your allies are your most important sources of support, because when other people believe in you, you can believe in yourself. It helps to have friends to back you up. I couldn't have done it without my friends.

—Kerry Pacer, White County High School
The Advocate Person of the Year, 2005

Step Two

Finding the right teacher to advise your GSA will be a crucial part of demonstrating to your principal that you have a well-thought-out plan. You probably already have a teacher in mind, so now's the time to ask. You might also consider asking one of your guidance counselors to act as a mentor for your GSA. Some guidance counselors have had special training on LGBT issues. They can do more than just fix your class schedule. They're also trained to provide students with tips and strategies for coping with difficult situations.

You also might consider having two advisors. When some of my students asked me to be their advisor, I thought it would be a good idea to have another teacher coadvise with me. Since I'm a gay male, I asked a straight female teacher to be the coadvisor. I thought we made a well-balanced combination, which kept up with the spirit of gay *and* straight alliance. Another added bonus was that she and I supported each other when things got crazy and angry parents were calling the school. And the fact that it wasn't just me that was the focus of the angry parents' attention helped too.

Steps Three Through Six

Steps three through six will vary from school to school. Most public schools, though, will require you to fill out a form any time you propose a new student club. The form will probably ask you to explain the goals and objectives of your club. What is it that you want to accomplish for the remainder of the school year? It might be helpful to divide activities into the following categories:

Social Activities

- Fund-raising for HIV/AIDS research or a battered-women's shelter
- Make different people in charge of coming up with a topic of the week
- Watch a video or news clip and discuss it
- Organize a dance or party
- Community service (for example, volunteer at a soup kitchen, collect canned foods, paint someone's house)
- Organize a BBQ, picnic, or movie night at someone's house
- Organize an LGBT Prom for schools in your area

Censorship

According to the U.S. Supreme Court case, *Board of Education, Island Trees v. Pico* (1982), your school cannot ban books from the library simply because they disagree with the information and ideas presented in them.

Educational Activities

- Work with your librarian to select appropriate LGBT-themed books for your library
- Organize panels of LGBT students to speak in classes or teacher in-services
- Invite speakers to the school from the community, a local house of worship, or a university
- Organize a book talk and signing with an author at your local bookstore
- Speak on a local or college radio show
- Celebrate National Coming Out Day on October 11 or Day of Silence in April (www.dayofsilence.org)
- Celebrate Transgender Day of Remembrance in November (www.gender.org/remember/day/index.html) or (www.gsa network.org/resources/dayofremembrance.html)
- Celebrate Intersex Awareness Day in October (www .intersex-awareness-day.org)
- Sponsor Gay and Lesbian History Month events
- Organize a Pride Week or LGBT Awareness event
- Host a GSA or Diversity Conference at your school
- Team up with other clubs in your school to promote awareness about racism, religious intolerance, and other forms of oppression
- Participate in a "Drop the Labels" campaign to end gender-based bullying and harassment in your school (www.gpac.org/youth/dtl)

- Put on a gay-themed play with the drama coach
- Make educational signs or posters to hang around the school
- Make an antiharassment or diversity appreciation video to show along with morning announcements

---

Safe Zone Poster Campaign

A fun and educational activity you can do in your school to raise awareness about bullying and harassment is to ask teachers if they would be willing to make their classrooms "safe zones" and to hang a Safe Zone poster in their room. The posters are available from the National Education Association and can be printed from their Web site at www.nea.org/schoolsafety/safezone.html

---

Political Activities

- Lobby your school board to adopt a nondiscrimination policy that includes sexual orientation and gender identity
- Organize a writing campaign addressed to your governor or members of Congress
- Hold a rally
- Meet with your area's elected officials
- Visit your state capitol and lobby lawmakers
- Network with other advocacy organizations such as the National Center for Transgender Equality (www.nctequality.org) and National Transgender Advocacy Coalition (www.ntac.org)

Once you've come up with a list of activities you'd like to do, you can use those as objectives or goals for your GSA. Once you prioritize activities, objectives, and goals that are the most important to your proposed GSA, then you can write a mission statement. If you've chosen mostly educational goals, then your mission statement should make it clear that one of the main purposes of your GSA is to educate others. Here's the mission statement my students agreed on, "The mission of the [name of school] Gay-Straight Alliance is to create an environment in which gay and straight people can respect and understand each other." Your mission statement can include some of your objectives, but it's usually best to keep it short and somewhat vague so that any objectives you think of down the road will fit in with the mission you've already created.

¡RECURSOS EN ESPAÑOL!

"Cómo Comenzar una Gay-Straight Alliance," de el Gay-Straight Alliance Network, *esta disponible en* www.gsanetwork.org/resources/recursos.html

"Fuera Del Clóset, Protegido/a y Respectado/a," de el Lambda Legal Defense and Education Fund, *esta disponible en* www.lambdalegal.org/cgi-bin/iowa/news/publications.html?record=1593

You also need to figure out who will be the officers for your club. The person who comes up with the original idea to start the GSA often wants to be president. The vice president helps out the president and takes over when the president can't come to a meeting. The secretary is usually in charge of keeping track of the membership list and taking minutes at the meetings. Minutes are a record of who attended, what you talked about, what was accomplished since the last meeting, and what you hope to accomplish by your next meeting. The treasurer is obviously in charge of the money and should check with your school's secretary about rules for collecting money at school. Remember, you can always hold elections at some later date to elect new officers and give other people the chance to lead the club. If your school allows it you can design your own leadership for the group, such as rotating facilitators, a steering committee, or some other model that distributes the power and decision making more equally among members.

When it comes to choosing a name, most GSAs opt for something like "The [name of your school here] Gay-Straight Alliance."

This is great and it reflects the important point about GSAs—that it's all about bringing gay and straight people together. Some other GSAs have chosen more personalized names and that's fine too. Some examples are Spectrum, OUT!, Pride, Project 10, and the catchy Gay and Straight People (GASP!).

Steps Seven Through Nine

Step seven, which involves preparing information on the 1984 Equal Access Act, is extremely important because your principal may be unfamiliar with GSAs and may not know that federal law requires him or her to treat your GSA just like any other club at your school. Being prepared with information for your principal will create a good impression, and will let your principal know that you are willing to work with him or her. Remember: Your principal can be a strong advocate, so be organized, professional, and cooperative. It's your principal who will be receiving phone calls from angry parents and news reporters and defending your legal right to form the GSA.

Since it's your principal's job to inform his or her boss of what's happening in the school, he or she will probably want to check with the superintendent and the school board. The school board will probably want to then consult the district's attorney. If your district's attorney has a good understanding of the law, he or she will counsel the school board to treat the GSA like any other student club. This process can take a while, and you'll need to be patient, yet persistent. That is, give your principal time and space to get the proper authorization but don't be afraid to check in with her or him often to see what progress is being made; just remember to do it politely.

Step Ten

Some people in your school and community might get angry once they find out you are starting a GSA. They may say nasty things to you and spread rumors, so you need to prepare for this

Letter to School Officials

The American Civil Liberties Union (ACLU) has made things easy for you. They have a letter, which you can print and give to your principal that explains your right to form a GSA. The letter is available at www .aclu.org/LesbianGayRights/LesbianGayRights.cfm?ID=9180&c=106

possibility. Who will you go to for support? It's good if you have support from your parents, but you can also get support from your friends, a teacher, your guidance counselor, an administrator, and people in the community. Most communities have local chapters of organizations for LGBT people and their allies. Some examples are Children of Lesbians and Gays Everywhere (COLAGE); Parents, Families, and Friends of Lesbians and Gays (PFLAG); Gay, Lesbian, Straight Education Network (GLSEN); a Safe Schools Coalition; or the American Civil Liberties Union (ACLU).

Many times, community members who don't want you to have a GSA will go to a school board meeting to protest. Students also have the right to speak at these meetings and explain why they want a GSA in their school. If you're comfortable doing this, it makes a strong impression in your favor. When school board members hear directly from students, they are more likely to support the GSA. But it's also a good idea to get adults to speak, especially your parents. Most of the gay supportive organizations (such as, PFLAG) have members who would be happy to come to school board meetings and speak on your behalf. You can also check with your local LGBT bookstore (if there is one), or a church, temple, or mosque in your area that is open and affirming of LGBT people, such as a Unitarian Universalist church or Reform Jewish Temple. Also, if you live near a university you can check if they have an LGBT student group on campus and you can ask them for support.

GETTING LEGAL HELP

If things get really ugly and you think you need the help of an attorney, you can contact one of the following organizations. These organizations will sometimes provide an attorney free-of-charge. You can also check with attorneys in your area to see if they'd be willing to represent you for free (pro bono).

Lambda Legal Defense and Education Fund

Call 212-809-8585 and ask for the Legal Help Desk or e-mail legalhelpdesk@lambdalegal.org

National Center for Lesbian Rights (NCLR)

Call 415-392-6257 or e-mail info@nclrights.org

American Civil Liberties Union (ACLU)

Visit their Web site at www.aclu.org to find the local chapter nearest you or contact the ACLU Lesbian and Gay Rights Project, at getequal @aclu.org

MAINTAINING A GAY-STRAIGHT ALLIANCE

Holding Regular Meetings and Membership

Once your GSA is approved, it's up to you to advertise for members and hold regular meetings. The GSA Network (www .gsanetwork.org) has listed great ideas for ways to get more members to attend your GSA meetings. Some of their ideas are to provide food, set up an information table at lunch, post flyers around the school, have an "open" meeting where you show a movie or have a guest speaker, create a display of LGBT-themed books in your library, or hold a "bring-a-friend day" meeting.

Many GSAs are started by straight students who are allies to LGBT people. This sends a powerful message that GSAs aren't just for LGBT students. In fact, the straight members sometimes outnumber the LGBT members and that's okay. Remember, though, that just because you started a GSA it doesn't mean that all the LGBT students in your school will want to join. Just as some straight students won't want to join the GSA, some LGBT students won't want to join the club either, and that's their choice. But, there are steps you can take to help make your GSA a safe and welcoming place for all types of people.

Youth Voices

I held the office of secretary in my high school's gay-straight alliance. The two co-presidents were both straight females and my two best friends. We sometimes joked that maybe the school thought we were some kind of lesbian trio, but we were pretty sure everyone knew that the GSA at our school was just a club, run by a bunch of liberal straight people. An interesting thing about our GSA, though, was that there were really only one or two openly gay members of the club, out of a little more than a dozen. We often wondered if some of our gay friends didn't join for that reason. We wondered if they were turned off to the club because they thought we paraded it as some sort of gay protection club. We also considered that because none of my openly gay friends were particularly chastised at our school, that maybe, they saw our club as unnecessary.

Michelle Melton
Fairfax County, VA

Including Disabled Students

It's important to remember that GSAs are for everyone, including *students who are disabled.* You can learn about issues important to LGBT people who are disabled by visiting www.queers OnWheels.com and enlisting the help of students in your school who have disabilities to make sure your GSA is truly accessible to everyone.

Including Transgender Students

GSAs are for transgender (or trans) people too. Trans students not only share many of the same concerns as lesbian, gay, and bisexual students, but also have many of their own concerns. For instance, some students do not identify as either male or female. You can put these students in an uncomfortable position if you call them by the wrong pronoun ("he" or "she"), plan an activity that requires males and females to separate, or if you have a form that requires students to check off either "male" or "female." To ensure you're making your GSA a safe and welcoming place for trans students, begin by educating yourself about what it means to be transgender. Then you can educate the rest of your school.

WHERE'S THE T?

"Jump-Start VIII: Where's the "T" in GSA? Making Your GSA Trans-Inclusive"

Online resources from GLSEN can help you make your GSA trans-inclusive. Available at www.glsen.org/cgi-bin/iowa/all/news/record/1737.html or e-mail them at jumpstart@glsen.org

"Beyond the Binary: A Toolkit for Gender Identity Activism in Schools"

This is an online resource from the GSA Network, which is designed to assist you in creating a safe space at your school for transgender and gender nonconforming students. Available at www.gsanetwork.org/BeyondtheBinary/toolkit.html

"Bending the Mold: An Action Kit for Transgender Youth"

This is an online resource from Lambda Legal and the National Youth Advocacy Coalition for transgender and intersex youth. It contains definitions, resources, and an action tool kit to help youth advocate for change. Available at www.lambdalegal.org/cgi-bin/iowa/news/publications.html?record=1504

Transgender Law & Policy Institute

News, resources, and legislation on transgender issues at www.transgenderlaw.org

Including LGBT Students of Color

When LGBT people and their allies form alliances with other disadvantaged and oppressed groups in society they can combine efforts and resources and work together for social justice and equality. White students must remember that students from different racial and ethnic backgrounds have different needs and experiences. LGBT students of color have to balance being a racial minority, on the one hand, with being a sexual minority on the other. They sometimes feel they have to choose between being a person of color or being an LGBT person. GSAs that form coalitions with other student groups who support human rights can make it easier for LGBT students of color to participate. Some ways you can create an atmosphere that welcomes LGBT students of color are:

- Use speaker bureaus and workshop facilitators who are racially diverse
- Decorate the meeting room with LGBT historical figures from many racial and ethnic backgrounds
- Have books, magazines, videos, and other materials that reflect different racial and ethnic LGBT people and groups
- Cosponsor school events with other student of color clubs, such as the Black Student Alliance or Mexican-American Student Club
- Cosponsor a multicultural task force with other racially and ethnically diverse student clubs and educate the school community about prejudice and discrimination (McCready, 2004)

YOUTH OF COLOR

"Youth Resource"

A project of "Advocates for Youth," provides this online resource with personal stories, peer educators, and other resources about GLBTQ youth of color. Available at www.youthresource.com/community/youth_of_color/index.htm

"Building Anti-Racist GSAs"

From the GSA Network, it has great ideas for coalition building. Check it out at www.gsanetwork.org/resources/pdf/Antiracist.pdf

"Jump-Start VI: Understanding Power, Privilege, and Oppression"

An online resource from GLSEN that can help the members of your GSA achieve a greater understanding of how to create a "less oppressive" and "more inclusive" student club for everyone. Available at www.glsen.org/cgi-bin/iowa/all/news/record/1629.html or e-mail them at jumpstart@glsen.org

SUMMARY

- Be prepared by doing your background research—use the resources.
- Get the support of your principal and a faculty advisor. Don't take "No!" for an answer.
- Get help from your parents, supportive adults in the community and teachers and students in your school. Let your voices be heard!
- Be inclusive of all students who want to participate. But also realize that some LGBT students won't want to join and that's their choice.
- Educate yourself about issues important to people who are transgendered, disabled, and people of color so you can include everybody.
- Design activities that engage students with different interests and have fun!

Chapter 3

For Teachers and Counselors: How to Work with GSAs

As a former middle and high school teacher, I understand first-hand the concerns many of us have when sexual orientation and gender identity issues come up in our schools. Currently, as a professor of education, I have learned that my preservice teachers' biggest fear is *not knowing* what they will be able to say or do when these issues come up in their own classrooms. Many of us have never received any training on this topic in our teacher education courses or in our district's in-services. This is changing for the better, however, as colleges of education and school districts realize the need for equipping teachers and counselors with the information and tools required to effectively address lesbian, gay, bisexual, and transgender (LGBT) issues in the classroom. Some educators are even lucky enough to work in districts that have made clear statements about valuing diversity by including sexual orientation and gender identity in their nondiscrimination policies.

But what about those of us who work in a district that has not yet taken a proactive stance? Although it is not within the scope of this book to teach you everything you need to know about sexual orientation and gender identity, I will provide you with a variety of resources and ideas you can draw on to educate yourself, which will enable you to network with and get support from others (Appendixes A and B).

Gay-Straight Alliances: A Handbook for Students, Educators, and Parents
© 2007 by The Haworth Press, Inc. All rights reserved.
doi:10.1300/5921_03

SEXUAL ORIENTATION
AND GENDER IDENTITY DEVELOPMENT

Many researchers believe that sexual orientation and gender identity formation are accelerated among contemporary youth, with many youth realizing their same-sex attractions at an early age. One of the latest and greatest resources on sexual orientation and gender identity development is:

Savin-Williams, Ritch C. (2005). *The New Gay Teenager.* **Cambridge, MA: Harvard University Press.**

An excellent resource with real case studies depicting how today's adolescents are rejecting traditionally defined labels like "gay" and "lesbian" and are forging their own unique sexual and gender identities, based on a more fluid and dynamic view of human sexuality.

A survey conducted by Parents, Families and Friends of Lesbians and Gays (PFLAG, 2005) reports that 95 percent of guidance counselors have little or no information for gay, lesbian, and bisexual youth or their parents and 99 percent have little or no information for transgender youth and their parents. It's up to all of us to educate ourselves, seek out others who share our conviction to help LGBT youth succeed in school, and arm ourselves with helpful resources, such as *Understanding Gay & Lesbian Youth: Lessons for Straight School Teachers, Counselors, and Administrators* by David Campos (2005) and *Gay-Straight Student Alliance Handbook: A Comprehensive Resource for Canadian K-12 Teachers, Administrators, and School Counselors* by Kristopher Wells (2006). Educators can also work with their professional associations to advocate the rights of LGBT students.

AMERICAN SCHOOL COUNSELOR
ASSOCIATION (ASCA)

The ASCA (www.schoolcounselor.org) has a members-only online resource center that includes links and suggested publications for school counselors working with LGBT students. They host sessions at annual conferences, which address the needs of LGBT students. The ASCA also worked with the National School Board Association to develop *Dealing with Legal Matters Surrounding Students' Sexual Orientation and Gender Identity,* available at www.nsba.org/site/docs/34600 /34527.pdf

For more information contact Jill Cook, Director of Programs, American School Counselor Association, 1101 King Street, Suite 625, Alexandria, Virginia 22314, Tel: 703-683-2722, Fax: 703-683-1619, or e-mail: jcook @schoolcounselor.org

WHERE TO BEGIN?

A good place to start when working with LGBT students and their allies is to avoid treating them as victims. It is also important to remember that their primary identification might be their religion, race, ethnicity, or some other characteristic, rather than their sexual orientation or gender identity. For instance, LGBT students with disabilities have different priorities than able-bodied LGBT students. The point is not to make a big fuss over sexual orientation and gender identity. Provide opportunities for them to celebrate who they are, no matter what their primary identification. Gay-straight alliances (GSAs) should be a place of celebration, an opportunity for all students to grow and develop into young adults, to blossom, and to be creative. Calling a GSA a "support group" holds negative connotations for many people. It's better to call it a student club. There's a time and a place for support and counseling for those students who are going through rough times, but try to avoid making the GSA all about helping LGBT students "get over their victimization." Instead, help LGBT students to realize and build upon their accomplishments and strengths, rather than focusing on how they are victims of oppression and bullying by straight and traditionally gendered society. A GSA will provide some support, no matter how it's structured. For instance, when LGBT students and their straight allies are allowed to have their own rituals (such as prom, special dances, movie nights, pizza parties, and other rites of passage), the youth feel safer and freer to express themselves. All of these opportunities provide developmental support that some LGBT youth don't receive elsewhere. Ultimately, however, the goal should be to make the school safe and welcoming enough where *all* students can participate in school functions together, rather than having separate proms and other special events.

Another helpful starting point is to maintain a broad view of adolescent gender identity and sexuality. This is one of the most critical areas in which parents and adults who work with youth remain uninformed. Don't force students to choose a sexual orientation or gender identity label. Allow them to define who they are, on their own terms, and in their own time. Or, respect their right to remain undefined.

NATIONAL EDUCATION ASSOCIATION (NEA)

- The NEA's Gay, Lesbian, Bisexual, and Transgender (GLBT) Caucus offers resources online at www.nea-glbtc.org
- The NEA offers several publications on all aspects of diversity, including, "Focus on Gays, Lesbians, Bisexuals, and Transgendered Persons."
- The NEA also offers training for educators on LGBT issues in education.
- For information on LGBT issues in education, contact Human and Civil Rights Division, 1201 16th St., NW, Washington, DC 20036-3290, Tel: (202) 822-7700, e-mail: hcrinfo@nea.org

AMERICAN FEDERATION OF TEACHERS (AFT)

- AFT has a Gay, Lesbian, Bisexual, and Transgender (GLBT) Caucus that meets every other year at the AFT's convention and stays in e-mail and newsletter contact.
- The caucus is also aligned with the United Federation of Teachers Special Project for members infected with and affected by HIV/AIDS. For more information, contact Pat Crispino at NJTPK8@aol.com or 212-598-9275.
- For general information on LGBT and other diversity issues in education, contact Constance T. Cordovilla, Associate Director Human Rights and Community Relations Department, American Federation of Teachers, 555 New Jersey Avenue, NW, Washington, DC 20001-2079, Tel: (202) 879-4490, FAX: (202) 393-8648, e-mail: ccordovi@aft.org

WORKING WITH LGBT STUDENTS OF COLOR

LGBT youth of color often have different concerns from their white LGBT peers. Religious beliefs and values, the importance of a tight-knit family, primary language, racial or ethnic identity, and other cultural factors can make coming out different for LGBT youth of color. Racial or ethnic identity, including being a nonnative English speaker, is often a more powerful identifier than one's sexual orientation or gender identity. Also, conservative religious beliefs are more prevalent in some ethnic minority and immigrant communities (Boykin, 1996). Thus, many LGBT Asian-American youth, for instance, feel more similar to straight Asian-Americans than to white LGBT people. Moreover, many LGBT youth of color report experiencing racism and discrimination in white-dominated GSAs and in community LGBT organizations (Cianciotto and Cahill, 2003).

Some GSAs are started by straight, white females who are allies of LGBT people. Their spirit is to be admired, but they sometimes don't understand the needs and concerns of LGBT students and students of color. McCready (2004) describes a "tendency of white female students [regardless of sexual orientation], like their black peers, to socialize with one another around a distinct set of racially-defined concerns, rather than build coalitions with students from different racial backgrounds, who may have an entirely different set of interests" (p. 45). Thus, special steps must be taken to make it okay for students to attend the GSA, even if their primary identity is not their sexual orientation or gender identity. One way of doing this is to build wide-ranging coalitions of students who can support a broad social justice agenda. (For more ideas, see the end of Chapter 2.)

BUILDING A DIVERSE GSA

Dr. Lance T. McCready, Assistant Professor of Education at Ontario Institute for Studies in Education, researches and writes about LGBT youth of color. He can be reached at lmccready@oise.utoronto.ca.

Dr. Kevin K. Kumashiro, Director of the Center for Anti-Oppressive Education, provides resources to challenge racism, sexism, and classism in schools. Visit www.antioppressiveeducation.org.

LGBT youth with disabilities should have access to GSAs too. For more information on LGBT youth with disabilities visit www.QueersOn Wheels.com.

WORKING WITH TRANSGENDER YOUTH

Dr. Brett Genny Beemyn, Board Member of the Transgender Law & Policy Institute, says that three main concerns for trans students are the harassment and violence they sometimes face, the stress and fear of having to use gender-segregated facilities or having to participate in gender-segregated groups or teams, and educators' and students' lack of understanding of trans issues, which may result in disrespectful treatment and discrimination (such as using the wrong name or pronouns, or expecting a trans person to behave or express themselves in certain gendered ways). One court prohibited a school from enforcing a dress code that did not allow the student to dress as the gender with which the student identified (*Doe v. Brockton School Committee*, 2000). Dominique Johnson researches trans issues in education and encourages school officials to provide trans students with appropriate gendered bathroom and locker room spaces and to change school records to reflect the student's gender identity.

Transgender Inclusivity

- Don't ask people to mark either "male" or "female" on forms
- If you separate boys and girls for activities, let them choose the group they want to work with
- Watch and discuss movies with gender nonconformist characters
- Discuss transgender people in the news

- Research statistics on transgender people and use those in your publicity materials
- Organize a campaign for a gender-neutral (unisex) bathroom at your high school
- Lead a gender sensitivity training for your school
- *My Gender Workbook,* by Kate Bornstein, offers many activities
- Don't make too huge an issue out of gender. Allow people to feel comfortable with who they are

Adapted from: www.gsanetwork.org/resources/pdf/Transgender.pdf

HELPING STUDENTS DEFINE THE PURPOSE OF THEIR GSA

According to the Federal Equal Access Act of 1984, student clubs must be initiated and run by students. Teachers and other school personnel can act as advisors to the group, however, and the students in your charge will probably need some guidance from time to time. One of the main challenges faced when starting a GSA is defining its purpose. As outlined in Chapter 2, some of the purposes of the GSA may be awareness, activism, education, socializing, and support. A broader perspective, however, can help define the club's purpose(s) at both the individual and institutional levels. Dr. Pat Griffin, Professor in the Social Justice Education Program at the University of Massachusetts, Amherst, contends that GSAs are good at addressing purposes at the individual level. For instance, GSAs combat antigay discrimination by becoming a visible presence in the school and by doing education for tolerance and school safety. This is a good place for a new GSA to start, but eventually, GSAs should become part of a larger institutional movement to change antigay curricula, policies, and practices of schools. That is, instead of settling for safety and tolerance, the GSA should help the school to become more socially just by addressing the ways in which the curriculum, policies, and practices of the school privilege heterosexuals and exclude LGBT students.

Griffin gives the following examples of changes a GSA could help institute in schools to bring about equality for LGBT students:

- A gender-neutral "public display of affection" policy that treats same-sex couples the same way as heterosexual couples.
- School-sponsored social events are open to same-sex couples and singles.
- Instead of a prom king and queen, students elect prom leaders of any sex or gender identity.
- Introduce gender-neutral dress codes.
- Forms and school literature are inclusive of all types of families, such as two moms or two dads.
- Other social justice–oriented clubs, such as the Martin Luther King Club, assume that some members are LGBT and include activities and interests directed at them.
- Teachers use inclusive language and do not assume heterosexuality and gender conformity.
- Staff development and student programming focuses on identifying heterosexism and heterosexual privilege.

LGBT-THEMED CURRICULA

GLSEN has many lesson plans in their Educator Library. Visit www
.glsen.org/cgi-bin/iowa/educator/library/curriculum.html

The Safe Schools Coalition also has free lesson plans online at www
.safeschoolscoalition.org/RG-lessonplans.html

HELPFUL TIPS
FOR WORKING WITH GSAs

A common complaint about GSAs is that they're "just a group of straight girls" (Mayo, 2004, p. 33). Griffin et al. (2004) report that in the GSAs they studied, many of the students who frequently attended were white heterosexual females, students who did not identify themselves, and students who didn't fit in any other cliques (regardless of their sexuality). As a result, some LGBT students seeking counseling and support don't see GSAs as safe places. One way around this is to have a separate support group only for students who identify as LGBT or "questioning" and have the GSA serve more social and educational purposes.

In districts where LGBT teachers and students consider it too risky to come out and have a GSA, one way they get around it is to meet privately and give their group an innocuous name that doesn't identify it as having anything to do with sexual orientation (such as Diversity Club). Another example is from a popular young adult fictional book by Brent Hartinger, in which a group of closeted gay high school students form their own club and name it the Geography Club so that no one will guess its true purpose.

Where possible, however, I recommend retaining the name "Gay-Straight Alliance." My advice is not to cave in to school officials who want a "less controversial" name. It's important to take a stand and let students know that *gay* is not a dirty word. Furthermore, where schools have asked GSAs to change their name, the courts have not looked favorably upon this practice because other student clubs were not asked to change their names (*Colín v. Orange Unified School District,* 2000). In working with your administration, it also helps to get the support of a local safe schools coalition or your local chapter of Parents, Families, and Friends of Lesbians and Gays (PFLAG) or Gay, Lesbian, Straight Education Network (GLSEN). Enlist the help of parents, clergy, and other community members to support and defend you and the students, especially if religious fundamentalist parents start to complain. You might also consider some sort of partnership with your district Health Coordinator, Director of Multicultural Education, or Office of Safe and Drug Free Schools for guidance, support, and funding. The No Child Left Behind Act requires, however, that if you use Safe and Drug Free Schools money to fund an education program that addresses "victimization associated with prejudice and intolerance" or "respect for the rights of others," then the school must make "reasonable efforts" to inform parents beforehand (Cianciotto, Cahill, and Johnson, 2005, p. 14).

Finally, it's important to keep in mind that GSA membership will ebb and flow over time as student leaders come and go and this is a natural process. It's important, however, to maintain regular meetings and a presence on campus, while at the same time, realizing that some years the GSA will accomplish great things and other years it may struggle to attract any members at all. One lesson I learned is that students need encouragement. Keep in mind, though, it's a fine line we, as educators, walk between encouraging students to be active in a GSA and pushing our own agenda onto them.

SUMMARY

- The club's advisor should ensure that straight allies feel comfortable attending the meetings and also that the concerns of lesbian, gay, and bisexual students, trans students, disabled students, and students of color are taken into consideration.
- Understand that for students with same-sex attractions, their primary identity may not be their sexual orientation.
- Some transgender students and students with same-sex attractions will not be comfortable joining the GSA and they should not be antagonized by students in the GSA for choosing not to attend meetings.
- Sometimes educators feel a stronger need for a GSA than do students. While it's okay to inspire students and let them know you will support them, there is a fine line between that and pushing your own agenda on them. Ultimately, it must be the students who initiate and run the GSA.

Chapter 4

For Principals and Superintendents: GSAs and the Law

Familiarity with the law can save a school district a large amount of money and a huge legal mess. Students who want to start gay-straight alliances (GSAs) are often more familiar with the law than are their principals. Students have access to reams of information on the World Wide Web and communicate via Internet chat rooms with other high school students all over the country who have successfully started GSAs in their own schools. Although this chapter explains school districts' responsibilities regarding GSAs, nothing I say in this book is meant to provide legal advice. If you have specific legal questions, you should seek the services of a qualified, licensed attorney.

FIRST AMENDMENT RIGHTS

The First Amendment of the U.S. Constitution provides the basic principles that guide courts' decisions on this and related issues. The First Amendment reads:

Congress shall make no law respecting an establishment of religion, or prohibiting the free exercise thereof; or abridging the freedom of speech, or of the press; or the right of the people peaceably to assemble, and to petition the Government for a redress of grievances.

Gay-Straight Alliances: A Handbook for Students, Educators, and Parents
© 2007 by The Haworth Press, Inc. All rights reserved.
doi:10.1300/5921_04

The founding fathers of the United States recognized the importance for individuals to be able to freely speak their opinions and to assemble with others of like mind. In 1969, the U.S. Supreme Court ruled in *Tinker v. Des Moines Independent School District* that the First Amendment applies to students and teachers in America's public schools as well. Though "freedom of association" is not spelled out in the First Amendment, the U.S. Supreme Court recognizes it as being "implicit in the freedoms of speech, assembly, and petition" (*Healy v. James,* 1972). Given these rights, students are able to seek affirmation of their personhood; to discuss and debate ideas, problems, and solutions with their peers; to form friendships; and to function as free and equal human beings. This is especially important for lesbian, gay, bisexual, and transgender (LGBT) students who are often denied the ability to speak freely or to associate with other LGBT students for fear of physical and emotional abuse by peers, and sometimes, by their own teachers, principals, and parents. GSAs provide a forum for students of all sexual orientations to speak freely on topics important to them and to associate with other like-minded students.

THE 1984 FEDERAL EQUAL ACCESS ACT

When it comes to GSAs, the most important law to be aware of is the 1984 Federal Equal Access Act (see Appendix C). This law was passed by Congress and signed by President Ronald Reagan in 1984, and ruled as constitutional by the U.S. Supreme Court in 1990 *(Board of Education of Westside Community Schools v. Mergens).* It states that if schools allow one noncurricular student club, then they must allow all clubs. If a school allows just one noncurricular club to meet on school grounds before, after, or during the school day, then this school is said, in legal terms, to have a *limited open forum.* According to the law, *all* noncurricular student clubs must be given equal access to this limited open forum. Noncurricular student clubs are those clubs that cannot be shown to relate directly to a school's curriculum, such as chess clubs and political or religious student clubs. On the other hand, French or Spanish clubs are curriculum-related as long as the school offers French and Spanish classes.

The Equal Access Act states that schools must allow noncurricular student clubs as long as the following criteria are met:

- Attendance at the meetings is voluntary.
- The club is student-initiated and student-run. A later court verdict (*Pope v. East Brunswick Board of Education*, 1993) also extended this to clubs that are faculty-initiated.
- School employees (such as teachers and counselors) cannot lead or participate in the meetings, although a school employee may act as a custodian of the group. (Most school districts require student clubs to secure a faculty advisor. If your district allows teachers or other school personnel to participate in noncurricular clubs in more than just a custodial capacity, however, then you should allow the same for a GSA.)
- People from the community may not regularly conduct or attend meetings that are held on school grounds. (Again, the club is to be student-led, free from outside influence. However, the club may invite guest speakers from the community.)
- And the club may not promote illegal activities, cause a substantial disruption, or interfere with other students' ability to participate in the school's educational activities.

Furthermore, the Equal Access Act has been interpreted by the courts to require that schools must treat all noncurricular student clubs equally. This means:

- The school must give all clubs equal access to funding, school newspapers, yearbook photos, meeting space, bulletin boards, and the public address system for announcing club meetings and activities (*Board of Education of Westside Community Schools v. Mergens,* 1990).

- Principals, counselors, and teachers have the right to monitor meetings as long as they do not participate.
- Schools can require student clubs to follow sets of rules, as long as the rules are applied equally to all clubs. Rules may include limits on meeting times and locations or nondiscrimination policies. One court, however, ruled that a religious student club could discriminate against persons of other faiths in selecting its officers. The court ruled that the club could limit leadership positions to students of certain faiths as long as the limitation was relevant to the message and purpose of the club (*Hsu v. Roslyn Union Free School District No. 3,* 1996).

In sum, the law requires that all noncurricular clubs be treated equally. Make sure your district's policies apply equally to all clubs and that the enforcement is equal. Making one exception or bending the rules for just one club opens the door to a claim of discrimination and a potential lawsuit.

A Brief History

The Equal Access Act was originally requested by Christian parents who wanted their children to be able to form religious student clubs (such as prayer and Bible study groups) that could meet on school grounds. Before this law, religious student clubs were often barred from meeting on school property because of concerns over violations of the First Amendment's establishment clause, which is commonly described as advocating *a wall of separation between church and state.* It was feared that if religious student clubs were allowed to meet on school campuses then it would send the message that the school officially endorsed the groups' religious views. There were also fears that opening the door to religious student clubs would eventually lead to proselytizing in school and mandated prayer over the public address system, both of which would clearly violate the separation of church and state.

In these cases, however, the courts ruled that religious speech is protected by the free-speech clause of the First Amendment and that schools cannot ban student clubs that are religious in nature simply because the school disagrees with the views of the club. Furthermore, the courts have ruled that simply allowing a club to meet on school grounds is not the same as officially endorsing the club's views. In other words, as long as the club confines its activities to outside the classroom, has voluntary attendance, and does not use class time to spread its views then it has the same right as any other club to use the school building for its meetings. Nowadays, much to the chagrin of religious fundamentalists, students are using this same law to petition their schools for the right to form gay-straight alliances.

Does it Apply to Elementary and Middle Schools?

So far, this law applies only to secondary schools. During the debates in Congress over the Equal Access Act, lawmakers feared that elementary and middle school students were not mature enough to initiate and lead religious clubs and that too much adult guidance and facilitation would be required. If teachers or administrators play any part in leading a noncurricular student club, then their participation could be seen as the school's official endorsement or sponsorship of that club. It is unclear whether middle schools may legally allow students to form religious or political clubs, although some do. Haynes, Chaltain, Ferguson, Hudson, and Thomas (2003), authors of *The First Amendment in Schools,* recommend that if a middle school allows students to form a religious or political club then the school should have a clear policy that is in line with the Equal Access Act, is applied equally to all noncurricular clubs, and makes clear that such student clubs are not sponsored or endorsed by the school.

Finagling the Law

One way that several districts have tried to get around the Equal Access Act and prohibit GSAs from forming in their schools is to prohibit *all* noncurricular student clubs. The big mistake these districts made, however, was to later allow some noncurricular clubs to sneak back into the school, either on the sly or by justifying the clubs as being curriculum-related, even though it was a stretch of the imagination to demonstrate some clubs' relation to the curriculum. The courts have not looked favorably upon this practice and have ordered the districts to allow the GSAs (*Boyd County High School Gay-Straight Alliance v. Board of Education of Boyd County*, 2003; *East High Gay/Straight Alliance v. Salt Lake City Board of Education*, 1999; *East High PRISM Club v. Seidel*, 2000). School districts that have always prohibited noncurricular clubs may be able to legally prevent a GSA from forming. As of yet, however, a case like this has not been tried in court. More important, any school district that considers the radical move of banning all noncurricular student clubs, just to prevent a GSA, should think twice about the repercussions. Many students rely on their participation in student clubs to help them obtain scholarships, not to mention the benefits of the educational opportunities and social activities that student clubs provide. This practice has been described as "cutting off one's nose to spite one's face."

Another way schools have tried to get around this law is to try to prove that the proposed student club would cause a *substantial disruption* to the school. GSAs sometimes cause headaches for school boards (with angry parents speaking at meetings), for administrators (who must field calls and e-mails from parents, the media, and other curious outsiders), and for teachers (who must take students' questions and facilitate contentious class discussions). Courts have not allowed instances such as these, however, as evidence that a student club is causing a substantial disruption (*Boyd County High School Gay-Straight Alliance v. Board of Education of Boyd County,* 2003). A potentially disruptive reaction from others (in response to a GSA) does not constitute a substantial disruption on the part of the GSA. A disruption from others in an attempt to stop a speaker or a group from exercising its First Amendment rights is known, in legalese, as the "hecklers' veto." Hecklers are those who attempt to intimidate speakers and groups with whom they disagree. Instead of banning a GSA because of fear of a negative community reaction, however, the courts advocate protecting the right of the GSA to meet, while addressing the concerns of angry parents as a separate issue. No doubt, this entails more work for school officials but it is the legal and just course of action.

Some school officials and parents have argued that the name, "Gay-Straight Alliance," is inappropriate and the students must choose a more innocuous name, such as "Tolerance Club" or "Alliance." Courts have not looked favorably upon this practice either, because other student clubs were not asked to change their names (*Colín v. Orange Unified School District,* 2000).

Other districts have tried to defeat the intent of the law by redefining curricular versus noncurricular clubs. In an interesting twist, Boulder Valley School District in Colorado had a policy prohibiting noncurricular student clubs, but at least one high school in the district allowed a GSA. The school argued that GSAs are related to the curriculum because sexual orientation is discussed in health classes. But when a group of students wanted to start a Bible club, their application was denied because the district's policy prohibited noncurricular clubs. Parents of those students threatened to sue and the district changed its policy (following the guidelines set forth in the Equal Access Act) to allow all noncurricular clubs.

Do Schools Have to Allow Neo-Nazi and Skinhead Student Clubs?

In the first place, the possibility that a group of students would make a request for such an offensive club is very slim. Second, student clubs petitioning for the right to meet on school property usually have to fill out a form outlining their purpose, goals, and objectives. While school officials cannot bar student clubs simply because they disagree with the viewpoint of their speech or the ideas they represent, student clubs that advocate violence, hate, and illegal activities can be excluded from the school. Thus, the cry that *anybody* will now be able to form a student club is a moot point.

In conclusion, school districts should stop trying to reinterpret the law in an attempt to prevent student clubs with which they disagree. It's a waste of time and money. The 1984 Equal Access Act clearly spells out which student clubs are permissible and under what conditions. Instead of wasting time and money trying to get around the law, schools should concentrate on educating students. School districts, by following the law and facilitating civil discussions on potentially controversial student clubs, can set a good example for students on how civilized adults behave in democratic and pluralistic societies.

THE EQUAL PROTECTION CLAUSE OF THE FOURTEENTH AMENDMENT

The Equal Protection Clause of the Fourteenth Amendment of the U.S. Constitution guarantees equal application of the law to all people, including students. A good example of how this law applies to LGBT students is the case of Jamie Nabozny, an Ashland, Wisconsin, student who sued his middle school principal, high school principal, and vice principal for almost one million dollars (*Nabozny v. Podlesny,* 1996). It was proven in court that these three administrators violated Nabozny's guarantee to equal protection in two ways. First, when Nabozny complained to his school administrators that he was the target of antigay harassment, he was told to fight back, whereas, harassment directed at female students was stopped. Thus, his school treated him differently because he is male and this gave rise to a claim of discrimination based on sex.

Second, it was proven that his school treated him differently because he is gay. This gave rise to a claim of discrimination based on sexual orientation. The court ruled that the three individually named principals discriminated against Nabozny by violating his right to equal protection under the law. An important lesson for principals is that they can be sued as individuals for failing to protect students from antigay harassment. The courts have also ruled that school boards can be held liable, in cases of severe and persistent peer harassment, where the abuse was reported and no actions were taken (*Davis v. Monroe County Board of Education,* 1999; *Ray v. Antioch Unified School District,* 2000).

TITLE IX

Title IX is a federal statute that prohibits sex discrimination in schools and has also been cited in cases of discrimination against LGBT students (*Henkle v. Gregory,* 2001). In one case, a gay male student alleged that he was abused in school because he did not conform to traditional male stereotypes. A court ruled that he was protected by Title IX's prohibition of discrimination based on sex (*Montgomery v. Independent School District No. 709,* 2000). Guidelines for developing a district's antiharassment policy, published by the U.S. Department of Education (1999), state that although Title IX does not prohibit discrimination on the basis of sexual orientation "Sexual harassment directed at gay or lesbian students may constitute unlawful sexual harassment." For instance, if a lesbian student is targeted for harassment by a male student or group of male students simply because she is lesbian, this is a case of sexual orientation discrimination. However, if the abuse directed at her is sexual in nature (that is, physical sexual advances) then this is also a case of sexual harassment and is prohibited by Title IX. Schools that fail to address and stop peer sexual harassment risk losing their federal Title IX funding.

Though the First Amendment, the Equal Protection Clause, and Title IX do not relate directly to GSAs, I mention them here because too many school districts learn the hard way that discrimination based on sexual orientation is unacceptable. In the end, it's better for everybody if school districts make the effort to respect the legal rights of all students. Doing so prevents the schools from costly lawsuits, increases student safety in the school, and provides students with important lessons on civility, rights, and democracy.

FREQUENTLY ASKED QUESTIONS

Do Religious Students Have the Right to Protest GSAs?

Students probably do have the right to protest a GSA in their school. Students who hold antigay religious views sometimes form their own religious student clubs, pass out literature about the ex-gay movement, and hold prayer meetings around the flagpole. School officials sometimes try to limit disruption to the school by trying to prevent any backlash on the part of religious students, but this can be a violation of their First Amendment rights. It is necessary, therefore, to review the guidelines for religious expression in public schools.

FEDERAL GUIDELINES FOR RELIGIOUS EXPRESSION IN PUBLIC SCHOOLS

1. Students have the same right to engage in individual or group prayer and religious discussion during the school day as they do to engage in other comparable activity.
2. Local school authorities have "substantial discretion" to impose rules of order but may not structure the rules to discriminate against religious activity or speech.

3. Students may attempt to persuade peers about religious topics as they would any other topics, but schools should stop such speech that constitutes harassment.
4. Students may participate in before- or after-school events with religious content, such as "see-you-at-the-flagpole" gatherings, on the same terms they can participate in other noncurricular activities on school premises.
5. Teachers and administrators are prohibited from either encouraging or discouraging religious activity and from participating in such activity with students.
6. Public schools may not provide religious instruction but may teach *about* religion.
7. Students may express their beliefs about religion in homework, artwork, and other written and oral assignments. The work should be judged by ordinary academic standards and against other "legitimate pedagogical concerns."
8. Students may distribute religious literature on the same terms as other literature unrelated to curriculum can be distributed.
9. Schools have "substantial discretion" to excuse students from lessons that are objectionable on religious or other conscientious grounds. But students generally don't have a federal *right* to be excused from lessons inconsistent with religious beliefs or practices.
10. Schools may actively teach civic values and morals, even if some of those values also happen to be held by religions.
11. Students may display religious messages on clothing to the same extent they may display other comparable messages.

Adapted from www.ed.gov/Speeches/08-1995/religion.html

Neutrality is the guiding principle that schools should follow in their treatment of students' freedom to express their religious points of view. Examples of neutrality are:

- Allowing students to express their antigay religious views as part of a class discussion, as long as their comments fit in the context of the discussion and are not said in a harassing or threatening manner
- Allowing Christmas decorations along with Hanukkah, Kwanzaa, and other religious and secular holiday symbols and decorations
- Allowing some religious songs, along with secular songs, in the winter concert

- Allowing students to hand out religious pamphlets before or after school, or during lunch
- Teaching about different religions in a comparative religions class

Examples that violate the principle of neutrality are:

- Preventing students from expressing their antigay religious viewpoints in class discussions just because the teacher or other students object
- Excluding any religious-themed music from being played in school concerts
- Preventing teachers from displaying Christmas decorations, as long as they are displaying decorations and symbols of other religious holidays and secular celebrations
- Preventing students from handing out pamphlets, just because they have a religious message
- Teaching that some religions are better than others in a comparative religions class.

An important point to remember is that squelching any expression of religion does not equal neutrality; it equals exclusion. Schools do, however, have the right to limit the time, place, and manner of students' expression of religious points of view, as well as any other points of view, as long as those limits are reasonable. School officials have the right to screen any materials that students distribute in school and can prohibit their distribution if the materials advertise or encourage illegal behavior, contain lewd or vulgar language, are sexually explicit, would cause a substantial disruption or true threat, or would violate the rights of other students (Haynes et al., 2003).

When it comes to students' religious expression before a captive audience, such as in the classroom or during a school-sponsored event, the law is not clear and has often deferred to the judgment of the school about when to limit students' free speech. Haynes et al. (2003) give the following advice:

> A general guide might be to allow students to express their religious views in a classroom or at a school event, as long as they don't ask the audience to participate in a religious activity, use the opportunity to deliver a proselytizing sermon, or give the impression that their views are supported or endorsed by the school. (p. 37)

When Does Student Free Speech Become Harassment or a True Threat?

Schools cannot ban student speech just because the ideas they present may be offensive or objectionable to some. When I was interviewing teachers and administrators during my doctoral work, I asked them to consider the following scenario: During class, the topic of homosexuality naturally arises as part of the class discussion. A student raises her hand and the teacher calls on her. She calmly states to the class, "I believe homosexuality is a sin and gays will go to hell." I then asked, "Is this harassment and how would you handle it?" The answers I got back ranged from, "No, it's not harassment—it's just her opinion," to, "It's definitely harassment, and that statement would not be tolerated." The responses of the teachers and administrators to this scenario had such a wide range that it does not speak too well of educators' understandings of First Amendment rights of students.

Though there are no hard and fast rules, but only guidelines, I believe a court of law would probably say that the student was simply expressing her opinion and was doing so in an appropriate manner. The student was not using profanity or "fighting words," she was not directing her comment at any one student, she was not pointing her finger or raising her voice, her comments fit within the context of the discussion, and she did not repeatedly bring up her comment. According to Haynes et al. (2003), student speech (written or oral) becomes harassment "when a student or group of students repeatedly intimidate or threaten another student, . . . interfere with a student's education, or disrupt the orderly operation of a school" (p. 69). In determining if student speech constitutes a true threat, courts consider the following factors:

> (1) the reaction of the recipient of the speech; (2) whether the threat was conditional; (3) whether the speaker communicated the speech directly to the recipient; (4) whether the speaker had made similar statements in the past; and (5) whether the recipient had reason to believe the speaker could engage in violence. (Haynes et al., 2003, p. 71)

In the example I gave, the student's speech does not fit any of these factors. Granted, some students in the class might become uncomfortable because of the student's remarks. The student's remarks might also present a challenge to the teacher, whose job is to ensure a safe and orderly classroom. But none of these concerns, in my opinion, warrant preventing the student from expressing her opinion. Likewise, other students in the class should then be allowed to give their opinions, as long as they do so in a nonharassing and nonthreatening manner. That is, they may critique ideas but not attack individuals.

The U.S. Department of Education (1999) offers guidelines for writing a district's antiharassment policy or "speech code." While schools can enact speech codes to try to prevent harassment, they cannot interfere with the First Amendment rights of students. Some schools' codes go too far in limiting student free speech. In *Saxe v. State College Area School District* (2001), the court ruled that the district's antiharassment policy, which forbids all offensive and hurtful language, was too broadly worded and violated the First Amendment. The U.S. Supreme Court, in Haynes et al. (2003), has pointed out, "the government may not prohibit the expression of an idea simply because society finds the idea offensive or disagreeable" (p. 70).

Do Teachers Have the Right to Speak Out Against GSAs?

The law is not clear on this matter. In school, teachers' First Amendment rights are slightly more restricted than students' rights, because "many courts are highly deferential to employer interests, especially public school officials" (Haynes et al., 2003, p. 94). Furthermore, if teachers were allowed to express their racist, antigay, or antireligious beliefs in the classroom it would create a threatening environment and would affect students' ability to participate fully in public education. However, this does not mean that school staff must agree that a GSA is a good thing. Teachers and other school employees are free to hold their own private opinions. Since a teacher's classroom is not a public forum, however, they probably do not have the right to express many of their personal opinions in school that they can otherwise express outside of school (Haynes et al., 2003).

If Your School Has a GSA Event or Diversity Training that Includes a "Pro-Gay" Message, Does Your School Also Have to Give Equal Time to an "Antigay" Message?

First, the distinction must be made between a club-sponsored event and a school-sponsored event. If your school's GSA is sponsoring an event (a speaker panel of LGBT people, for instance) then they are probably not required to offer an opposing point of view (by also inviting antigay speakers to sit on the panel). In the interest of preserving First Amendment rights, however, if the GSA is allowed to have an event such as this then the school should not deny another club's request to have a similar event with an opposing point of view.

When it comes to school-sponsored events, however, it is a different story. If the school were to offer an antiharassment training that put homosexuality in a neutral or positive light, then the school is probably not required to offer an opposing view. Courts have usually given schools substantial discretion in determining the content of their curricula and trainings.

Where schools have encountered problems, however, is when they begin to mix religious points of view with the curriculum and assemblies. For instance, in *Hansen v. Ann Arbor Public Schools* (2003), the court ruled in favor of a student who sued her school for refusing to allow her to present her religious view that homosexuality is immoral and sinful. The school allowed its GSA to handpick a speaker panel for a discussion on homosexuality and religion. All the speakers, who were chosen by the GSA and approved by the school, were clergy representing religions with pro-gay beliefs. School officials rejected the student's request to pick a clergy with antigay beliefs or to sit on the panel herself. The court decided that because the clergy were handpicked by the school, the panel did not have a secular purpose, and limiting the panel only to pro-gay clergy suggested that the school endorsed a particular religious point of view.

Similarly, in *Citizens for a Responsible Curriculum v. Montgomery County Public Schools* (2005), the court ruled in favor of a community group protesting a revised sexual education curriculum that included the viewpoints of pro-gay religions to the exclusion of antigay religions, believing the curriculum may be in violation of the establishment clause of the First Amendment. For instance, the curriculum praises various religions that are open and affirming of LGBT people but portrays religions with antigay views as being intolerant. The court's decision reads, in part,

> The Court does not understand why it is necessary, in attempting to achieve the goals of advocating tolerance and providing health-related information, Defendants must offer up their opinion on such controversial topics as whether homosexuality is a sin, whether AIDS is God's judgment on homosexuals, and whether churches that condemn homosexuality are on theologically solid ground.

It seems that when schools introduce religion into school-sponsored discussions or curricula, and position pro-gay religions against antigay religions, it can give rise to claims of discrimination. The establishment clause of the First Amendment says government cannot favor one religion over another. Public schools, as extensions of the government, should not allow only pro-gay religions to present their side of the story while excluding antigay religions; schools must remain neutral when it comes to religion. To avoid this, schools should choose secular speakers and avoid school-sponsored speech that analyzes the rightness or wrongness of various religions. If religion comes up in a panel discussion, it may be okay as long as the invited panel of speakers (as a group) is not pushing one religion's view over another because that can be construed as school endorsement of that particular religious point of view. And, of course, students have the right to express their opinions on the topic, no matter that some people might find them offensive, as long as they do so in a manner that is nonharassing and nonthreatening. A guiding principle, which schools might follow in deciding what types of school-sponsored speech to allow, is to ask the question "Is the point of view democratic or theocratic?" It is well within the purpose of public schools to advance democratic points of view. Discussions regarding which religion is right or wrong have no place in school-sponsored activities and are best left to students and their parents.

SUMMARY

- The 1984 Equal Access Act states that if a school district allows noncurricular clubs then they cannot prohibit a GSA.
- Some school districts try to finagle their way around the law, but this often results in costly lawsuits. A better use of time and money is to honor the students' right to form the GSA and educate the school and community members who oppose it.

- The Freedom of Speech clause and Assembly clause of the First Amendment speak to the importance of providing safe spaces (such as GSAs) in which groups of students can assemble and speak about topics of importance to them.
- The Equal Protection Clause of the Fourteenth Amendment has been cited in court cases where school administrators did not stop antigay abuse directed at LGBT students. School districts risk losing their Title IX funds if they do not stop peer sexual harassment of all students, including LGBT students.

Chapter 5

For School Boards: Understanding the Opposition and Working with Parents

School board members often find themselves caught in the middle of battles over gay-straight alliances (GSAs), which spill out of the schools and into the community. This chapter addresses the reasons why some parents oppose GSAs and how school boards can most effectively manage the resulting debate.

An important point to keep in mind is that most parents want schools to address lesbian, gay, bisexual, and transgender (LGBT) issues. A 2001 survey of parents' attitudes "found that 80 percent of parents favor expanding existing antiharassment and antidiscrimination policies to include [LGBT] students [and] support teacher sensitivity trainings on tolerance that include instructions on dealing with gay and lesbian harassment in schools." Furthermore, "63 percent favor including positive information about gay and lesbian people in middle and high school health and sex education classes [and] 60 percent favor information about transgender people in those forums" (GLSEN, 2006). It is a minority of religious fundamentalist parents who oppose LGBT issues in schools, however, who protest the most by writing letters, sending e-mails, making phone calls, and speaking at school board meetings. Why do some religious fundamentalist parents see a GSA as such a threat and expend so much time and energy opposing it? To fully

Gay-Straight Alliances: A Handbook for Students, Educators, and Parents
© 2007 by The Haworth Press, Inc. All rights reserved.
doi:10.1300/5921_05

understand the answer to this question, we must begin with the fundamental beliefs and worldviews of religious fundamentalists regarding sexuality.

UNDERSTANDING THE OPPOSITION

Religious fundamentalists believe in a morally correct way of life, the foundation of which is their religion. Two of their main concerns are to raise their families in accordance with their religion and to instill in their children certain religious beliefs and moral values. Any group or institution that affects their parental right to raise their children as they see fit is seen as a grave threat.

Religious fundamentalists believe in God-given truths, for which there are no compromises. Among their core beliefs are that men naturally love women and vice versa. The concept of having a sexual orientation is foreign to many of them. They don't see themselves as having or belonging to a heterosexual orientation. That they are sexually and romantically attracted to the opposite sex is tacitly assumed and, because it seems natural and normal to them, it therefore goes unquestioned. To even bring up the topic of sexual orientation begs the question that such a thing as different sexual orientations exists, which they do not believe.

Rather, they believe that human beings are naturally attracted to the opposite sex, and that LGBT people are simply acting out on unnatural temptations, which must be overcome through prayer and a firm belief in God. When schools allow GSAs to form, religious fundamentalists believe it sends the message that the school officially endorses homosexuality as an acceptable alternative to heterosexuality. According to their beliefs, the only mention of homosexuality should be to say it is wrong.

Claims of Legitimating and Promoting Homosexuality

Religious fundamentalists claim that GSAs "legitimate and promote homosexuality." They fear the school's resulting treatment of homosexuality inside and out of the classroom will send the message, "It's okay to be gay." They believe that when schools allow GSAs, and students are permitted to discuss homosexuality openly, the result will be to *legitimize* homosexuality as normal and *promote* homosexuality as being just as good as, or equal to, heterosexuality (Macgillivray, 2004, 2005). A devout Mormon and mother of school-aged children, whom I'll call Carol, told me, "I do not want anyone telling [my children] that this is an alternative lifestyle that is acceptable and okay and just another choice. That's completely against my religion."

Thus, when their children's school allows a GSA and treats discussions of homosexuality in a neutral manner, religious fundamentalists feel they are being forced to agree with something with which they strongly disagree. Furthermore, it makes it more difficult for them to teach their children that homosexuality is wrong. When they protest, they feel it makes them look like bigots in the eyes of more tolerant and liberal parents and students. Carol, after sharing her antigay beliefs at a school board meeting, said, "I've felt a feeling of condescension, that because I'm trying to live a moral life in accordance with my conscience and the outlines that God has given in the scriptures and that I'm some kind of a narrow-minded bigot."

REVERSE DISCRIMINATION?

The end result is that religious fundamentalists end up feeling they are being discriminated against because the school is not siding with their beliefs. They sense this change in all areas of society, from bans on school-sanctioned prayer and the teaching of evolution to the legalization of abortion. They feel caught in a "culture war" and believe that if American society does not return to fundamentalist Christian values, moral decay will lead to the destruction of their way of life (White, 2006). Thus, religious fundamentalists often feel they are fighting a war for their very existence. Carol explained to me,

> I'm a student of history and in every other society where homosexuality became normal and accepted and just another lifestyle that was one of the signs of its eventual collapse. I don't like what is happening to the family today. I live my life thinking about my grandchildren and great grandchildren and what kind of a life are they going to live? I think for the sake of holding onto the things that I hold dear, morality and a belief in God, that I simply had to speak [at the school board meeting].

Religious fundamentalists have a right to their beliefs. They also have the right to instill their beliefs in their children. Where their rights end, however, is where the rights of other parents and students begin. Many parents support GSAs. Moreover, LGBT students have the same right as religious fundamentalist students to have their identities acknowledged and affirmed in the school. The intent of laws such as the 1984 Equal Access Act is to balance the rights of all sides by allowing all student clubs, even the ones with which we may personally disagree.

COMMON ARGUMENTS AGAINST GSAs

Religious fundamentalists have realized over the years that using religious arguments to oppose GSAs leaves them looking intolerant. Thus, they have become savvy in selecting their arguments and nowadays often rely on libertarian themes of parental autonomy and government nonintervention to make their case (Macgillivray, 2004). The old arguments, such as "God created Adam and Eve, not Adam and Steve," are no longer taken seriously, and religious fundamentalists have revised their approach to use arguments that appear to be fair at face value. When scrutinized within legal and democratic frameworks, however, their arguments do not hold up and are designed to protect only their own interests.

In cases where school boards have adopted policies that affirm the rights of LGBT students or have allowed GSAs to form, religious fundamentalist parents have countered with arguments such as:

- The school is promoting/endorsing homosexuality.
- GSAs are sex clubs. Students shouldn't be talking about sex.
- GSAs are "gay recruitment clubs."
- GSAs will cause a disruption to the school.
- GSAs undermine parents' ability to teach their kids that homosexuality is wrong.
- Students and teachers are being "forced to agree with homosexuality."

WHY THE COMMON ARGUMENTS ARE FALSE

Here I address each aforementioned argument and explain why it does not hold up under scrutiny. The frequently used argument that the school is "promoting homosexuality" is often misunderstood. When religious fundamentalists use this phrase, they do not mean that the school is *celebrating* homosexuality and telling everyone they should be gay. Rather, it means that the school is treating homosexuality in a neutral fashion, whereas heretofore, it has remained unmentioned or was treated only in a negative fashion. Religious fundamentalists don't want homosexuality to be acknowledged as a legitimate sexual orientation or treated neutrally. Promoting homosexuality does not mean elevating it to a *higher* level than heterosexuality, rather, it means elevating it to the *same* level as heterosexuality. Although this would be the fair and neutral course of action, religious fundamentalists want to preserve their own interests and stop any discussions of homosexuality in the school. When homosexuality is discussed, they want it cast only in a negative light. They do not want their kids to get the message that homosexuality is just as acceptable as heterosexuality. In fact, religious fundamentalist parents have been successful at passing *No Promo Homo* laws and policies in the states of Alabama, Arizona, Mississippi, South Carolina, Texas, and Utah. The laws prohibit any discussion of homosexuality in schools or mandate that homosexuality be referred to only in a negative manner.

For many religious conservatives, the word "gay" connotes sex. Thus, they reason, one cannot talk about being gay without talking about sex. This is not the case, however. Heterosexual, homosexual, and bisexual people alike talk about their sexual orientations all the time without mentioning sex. For example, one need not mention sex in describing a wedding, a date, a family vacation, or what one's family did over the weekend. The point is that students of all sexual orientations can come together in a GSA and discuss their personal lives, school activities, or fund-raising ideas without the discussion being sexual in nature. Even if the topic of sex does come up, it should not matter since sex-related topics also arise in classes and other student clubs. Moreover, courts have ruled there is no reason to believe that high school students are unable to manage discussions of sex (*Colín v. Orange Unified School District,* 2000).

Another frequent argument used to try to prevent GSAs is that they will cause a disruption in the school. However, a disruption from rowdy students or angry parents in reaction to a GSA is not the same as a disruption from the GSA. While a GSA may spark controversy in the school and the community, courts have not allowed this as a sufficient reason to ban a GSA from forming. The courts have ruled that schools must protect the rights of students to form a GSA, even if others in the school or community protest (*Boyd County High School Gay-Straight Alliance v. Board of Education of Boyd County,* 2003). It is the school's responsibility to make it possible for the GSA to peaceably assemble and to deal with protestors as a separate issue.

Arguments that GSAs are "recruitment clubs" are unfounded when one considers the research and literature on human sexual orientation. This argument stems from religious fundamentalists' belief that there is no such thing as a homosexual *orientation*, and people who claim to be lesbian, gay, or bisexual have been indoctrinated. Similarly, they believe one can "get over" one's homosexuality with the help of ex-gay ministries who use so-called "reparative therapy." Ex-gay ministries and reparative therapy, however, have been denounced by the American Psychological Association, the American Medical Association, and other professional organizations.

The Ex-Gay Myth

Wayne R. Besen, author of *Anything But Straight: Unmasking the Scandals and Lies Behind the Ex-Gay Myth* (2003, The Haworth Press), went undercover, posing as a gay man who wanted to change and was able to study the inner workings of ex-gay ministries. He gives countless examples demonstrating reparative therapy as a sham. One technique, he reports, is that participants wear a rubber band around their wrist and snap themselves when they have "gay thoughts." Besen's book exposes how ex-gay ministries lie and deceive to raise money and justify their existence.

Claiming that the school is "endorsing" a certain value, especially a value that runs counter to their beliefs, is also a frequent argument of religious fundamentalists. By allowing GSAs to meet, however, schools are simply following the letter of the law and giving all groups equal access to the school's limited open forum. One could make the same charge that the school is endorsing religion when it allows a Bible club. But the courts have ruled that schools are not endorsing a particular religion or point of view, as long as other religions or points of view are not excluded, which is the purpose of the 1984 Equal Access Act.

Finally, the charge that teachers and students are being forced to agree with homosexuality does not stand up under scrutiny. Under the First Amendment, everyone has the right to hold and express whatever opinions he or she wants, given certain constraints. Just because the child of religious fundamentalists may be part of a class discussion on homosexuality, does not mean the child will be forced to agree that homosexuality is okay. Students in public schools learn about all sorts of different cultures, nationalisms, creeds, religions, and peoples. Learning about a religion, for instance, is not equivalent to being forced to agree that the religion is good, right, or the best one. It is the school's job to present a variety of perspectives, and students are free to make up their own minds and form their own beliefs with the guidance of their parents. If the child of religious fundamentalist parents comes to believe "It's okay to be gay," it's because the child arrived at that conclusion on his or her own, not because he or she was coerced into that belief. This is the very possibility, however, that religious fundamentalist parents want to prevent. Thus, when they try to prevent GSAs, they don't see it as violating other peoples' rights. They see it only as preservation of their own.

STRATEGIES FOR WORKING
WITH THE OPPOSITION

Given that religious fundamentalist parents have entrenched beliefs in an absolute truth, how does a school board try to appease both advocates and opponents of GSAs? Unfortunately, because religious fundamentalists' beliefs are so rigid there is frequently little or no compromising, and they often feel discriminated against when school boards don't bow to their wishes. Richard, another parent I interviewed, opposed the inclusion of sexual orientation in a district policy. After speaking at a board meeting, he explained, "Most of the parents, once they said their piece and lost [when the school board adopted the policy, despite opponents' objections], have basically given up. I hear more of that group threatening to pull their kids [out of the public schools]. They're fed up." Frank, another parent, stated, "It seems okay to discriminate against Christians."

Let the Opposition Voice Their Concerns

One simple strategy that school boards can use is to give the opposition the opportunity to voice their concerns, and then listen to them. In the fall of 2004, high school senior, Eric Pérez formed the first GSA in his school district. Following approval of the GSA by the district and the GSAs first meeting, two school board meetings were filled beyond capacity with both supporters and opponents, who extended the community input portions of the meetings well beyond their usual time allotments. The school board sat patiently and listened to all those who wished to speak. Though the board knew it had to follow the law and allow the GSA, opponents were given the opportunity to be heard and this was the best the school board could offer them. The issue did not arise at subsequent school board meetings. Now, two years later, it is forgotten.

Engage Both Advocates and Opponents in Dialogue

In another district, the school board held special work sessions and invited parents who opposed the district's inclusion of sexual orientation in a policy to voice their concerns. Furthermore, a community group that advocated for the policy met with the religious fundamentalist parents, and this meeting helped both sides feel they were being taken seriously. The meeting took place in a church, which donated its space, and the two groups discussed their concerns and collaborated on a letter to the school board highlighting their areas of agreement on the policy. Dorothy, the leader of the group advocating the policy, explained that the meeting and the resulting letter were "done to give some satisfaction to the opposition. They needed to be heard and to be taken seriously. We let them vent their feelings and we listened without arguing." One of the religious fundamentalist parents later commented on that meeting:

> What I liked was that we sat down together as individuals and we actually spoke to one another, instead of being in a large room speaking at a podium [after months of the two groups opposing one another at school board meetings]. We had a discussion and I came out of it with a great deal more respect and understanding where they were coming from. It didn't change my religious conviction, didn't change my point of view. I just had greater understanding, which is what we really want with this deliberative process, where we can sit down and talk to people and understand where they were coming from, without changing who we thought we are. And by doing that, by having that better understanding, we can make changes in the community that are positive, that are for everybody.

Meeting with the supporters of the policy and collaborating on a letter of agreement to the school board helped relieve the opposing parents' concerns. By meeting and listening to one another's concerns, both sides came away feeling less mistrust and animosity toward the other. Even though the meeting and resulting letter did not change the school board's decision, or either sides' convictions for or against the board's policy, it did help to provide an appropriate outlet for democratic deliberation and allowed both sides to speak and to hear the other so they could feel better about moving on.

Draw on Community Resources

Many communities have local chapters of organizations that are happy to volunteer their time and make presentations to school boards, opposing parents, and other community groups. These organizations include Parents, Families, and Friends of Lesbians and Gays (PFLAG); Gay, Lesbian, Straight Education Network (GLSEN); American Civil Liberties Union (ACLU); local safe schools coalitions; and others. Many churches, synagogues, and mosques have clergy, rabbis, or imams who advocate safety and inclusion for LGBT students and who are willing to cultivate understanding between religious fundamentalist parents and supporters of GSAs. Whenever possible, it is also a good idea to include LGBT parents or parents of LGBT students.

FIND A CHAPTER NEAR YOU

Gay, Lesbian, Straight Education Network (GLSEN)
www.glsen.org

Parents, Families, and Friends of Lesbians and Gays (PFLAG)
www.pflag.org

Children of Lesbians and Gays Everywhere (COLAGE)
www.colage.org

Family Pride
www.familypride.org

American Civil Liberties Union (ACLU)
www.aclu.org/LesbianGayRights

Soul Force
www.soulforce.org

Welcoming Christian Church Directory
www.gaychurch.org/Find_a_Church/find_a_church.htm

Stick to Important Issues for Which There Can Be a Resolution

Don't get sidetracked and bogged down in arguments that are based on personal opinion or religious belief. Although it is important to allow opposing parents to voice their concerns, many of which will be based on their religious beliefs, it is not helpful to try to change their religious and personal beliefs. The important points that both sides should accept are: (1) if the district allows noncurricular clubs, then it must allow a GSA and (2) parents who oppose GSAs may be able to prohibit their child from attending one, but they do not have the right to prevent other peoples' children from attending one.

Student safety is often a powerful argument in building support for GSAs or school policies that affirm and acknowledge the rights of LGBT students. Religious fundamentalists, too, support the idea that all students should be safe in school, free from harassment and bodily harm. Demonstrating that GSAs are one way to enhance school safety for students, based on their real or perceived sexual orientation and gender identity, may help to build understanding with the opposition.

Student Voices Are Powerful

Where school board meetings are consumed by debates over GSAs, they should invite students to speak on their own behalf. This is one of the most effective strategies in building support for any change in school that involves sexual orientation and gender identity issues. I have attended numerous school board meetings where students eloquently and fearlessly gave accounts of antigay abuse they and their friends have suffered in their schools, and have explained how a GSA can help improve the school climate. Religious fundamentalist parents often charge that students are being manipulated and indoctrinated by outside forces with a radical pro-gay agenda. Allowing students to personally address those parents' concerns turns that claim on its head. Furthermore, by including students in the democratic process, they learn important lessons about civic participation.

ONLINE RESOURCES

Public Schools and Sexual Orientation: A First Amendment Framework for Finding Common Ground, a joint publication by American Association of School Administrators, Christian Educators Association International, and others, is available from the First Amendment Center's Web site at www.firstamendmentcenter.org/PDF/sexual.orientation.guidelines.PDF

Just the Facts about Sexual Orientation and Youth, is available from the American Psychological Association's Web site at www.apa.org/pi/lgbc/facts.pdf

SUMMARY

- Listen to the oppositions' concerns.
- Get advocates and opponents to talk with one another.
- Draw on the expertise of organizations, religious establishments, or individuals in the community.
- Build support for the GSA by showing how it can help enhance school safety.
- Invite students to speak at school board meetings.

School boards can rarely appease both sides in any debate, especially when deeply entrenched religious beliefs are involved. School boards must follow the law (in this case the 1984 Equal Access Act) or they risk being sued. The board must allow the GSA even though religious fundamentalist parents feel their rights are being violated. Although the school board can try to convince religious fundamentalist parents that the schools must remain neutral in their treatment of different student clubs, chances are that religious fundamentalists' opinions will not be altered, and they will go away feeling their rights and religious beliefs are not being respected. For this, there is no remedy. As long as they believe they hold the truth and attempt to infringe upon other peoples' rights in order to protect their own self interests, they will feel that their own rights are being violated.

Chapter 6

For Parents:
Supporting Your Child

Losing the love and support of their parents is one of the biggest fears of teens who are transgender or have same-sex attractions. Though homosexuality is not the taboo subject it once was, and many parents are supportive of their trans children and children with same-sex attractions, it is still difficult to "come out" to parents and have discussions about sexuality and gender identity. I came out to my parents when I was a senior in high school. I didn't want to live a lie any longer (pretending that I was straight), but I feared my parents might reject me and throw me out of the house, as had happened to a few other people I knew. Luckily, for me, my parents told me, "We love you and you will always be our son." That was just what I needed to hear, and those simple words erased a mountain of burden I had been carrying on my back for years. Nowadays, many resources are available to parents of children with same-sex attractions or nontraditional gender identities, Parents, Families, and Friends of Lesbians and Gays (PFLAG) being one of the most widely known.

Gay-Straight Alliances: A Handbook for Students, Educators, and Parents
© 2007 by The Haworth Press, Inc. All rights reserved.
doi:10.1300/5921_06

**PARENTS, FAMILIES, AND FRIENDS OF LESBIANS
AND GAYS (PFLAG) www.pflag.org**

PFLAG Transgender Network
Available at www.youth-guard.org/pflag-tnet

**"Faith in Our Families: Parents, Families, and Friends Talk
About Religion and Homosexuality"**
Available at www.pflag.org/fileadmin/user_upload/FaithinourFamilies.
pdf

You can find the nearest local PFLAG chapter by going to
www.pflag.org/index.php?id=189
or by contacting their national headquarters at
PFLAG National Office
1726 M Street, NW
Suite 400
Washington, DC 20036
Main Phone: (202) 467-8180
Fax: (202) 467-8194
E-mail: info@pflag.org

PFLAG has local chapters in communities across the country
and offers support groups for parents, family members, and friends
of lesbian, gay, bisexual, or transgender (LGBT) people. Their
Web site also offers many free publications. PFLAG offers gentle
support, without pressure, from caring individuals who have LGBT
members of their own families.

RESOURCES FOR PARENTS OF LGBT CHILDREN

*Trans Forming Families: Real Stories about Transgendered Loved
Ones* (2003), edited by Mary Boenke. Personal stories that help family
members understand being transgender.

*Always My Child: A Parent's Guide to Understanding Your Gay, Les-
bian, Bisexual, Transgendered, or Questioning Son or Daughter*
(2002), by Kevin Jennings and Pat Shapiro. It contains real-life stories,
scientific research, and practical advice to help parents support their
LGBT children.

Is It a Choice? Answers to 300 Most Asked Questions About Gay and Lesbian People (1999) by Eric Marcus. For parents whose children have just come out to them.

Loving Someone Gay (1997) by Don Clark. Written by a gay psychologist who works with gay people and their families.

Straight Parents, Gay Children (1999) by Robert A. Bernstein. From the parent of a lesbian child who explains his process of coming to terms with his daughter's sexual orientation.

Harmful to Minors: The Perils of Protecting Children from Sex (2002) by Judith Levine. The best book on human sexuality I have ever read. The author cuts through the rhetoric and myths around adolescent sexuality and gives forthright information based on research.

What Does Gay Mean? An online resource from the National Mental Health Association for parents about how to talk to kids about sexual orientation and gender identity. Available at www.nmha.org/whatdoes gaymean

Transfamily. An online resource offering support to transgender people, their parents, partners, children, and other family members. Available at www.transfamily.org

There are also numerous books for both parents and teens. A final point to remember is that just because your child has started a gay-straight alliance (GSA) or is a member of one, does not mean he or she is LGBT. In fact, many teens who are involved in GSAs identify as heterosexual. Their reasons for joining a GSA might be to show support for their LGBT friends, practice civil involvement in a worthy cause, or just to be with their friends who are involved in one. Whatever the reason, GSAs, like any student club, are a great way to get involved and work for positive change in one's school and community.

RESOURCES FOR LGBT TEENS

GLBTQ: The Survival Guide for Queer and Questioning Teens (2003) by Kelly Huegel. An excellent resource for GLBTQ children and their parents containing true stories and first-person comments from happy and well-adjusted GLBTQ young people.

When the Drama Club Is Not Enough (2001) by Jeff Perotti and Kim Westheimer. Contains moving stories and practical strategies for change and garnering support for safe schools initiatives.

Growing Up Gay in America (2002) by Jason R. Rich. Topics from coming out to sex are dealt with in an explicit and straightforward manner.

Web sites:
www.youthresource.com
www.gayteens.org
www.YoungGayAmerica.com
www.OutProud.org
www.AdvocatesForYouth.org

BALANCING PARENTS' RIGHTS WITH THOSE OF THE PUBLIC SCHOOLS

Unfortunately, not all parents support their children who are same-sex attracted or are differently gendered, nor do they respect other students' rights to form clubs based on their interests. Whenever students form GSAs, or any time schools present students with factual information on human sexuality, religious fundamentalist parents are usually the first to object. Parents have the right to instill their beliefs in their children and to participate in their children's education. But parents do not have the right to insist that public schools teach their beliefs to the exclusion of others.

Public schools are given substantial discretion to set their own curriculum and policies. Generally, any class or instructional activity, which is part of the district's mandated curriculum, is required and can be difficult to get out of, unless parents have a religious objection (Haynes et al., 2003). However, most states have "opt out" provisions, which give parents the right to remove their children from certain activities, such as Family Life Education, or any assembly or instructional activity that is not related to the mandated curriculum.

From a practical standpoint, schools usually work with parents to arrive at some reasonable compromise that neither disrupts the curriculum nor violates the parents' beliefs, rather than battle with them at every turn. For instance, even though parents do not have an absolute right to access classrooms, most schools allow parents to visit classrooms and sit in on lessons for limited periods of time. Also, parents can request that their child be assigned to—or away from—particular teachers or classes. Although a school cannot unreasonably deny such a request, it does not have to honor it, if it would affect another student's assignment.

Under the "unsafe school choice option" of the No Child Left Behind Act (NCLB), schools that are persistently unsafe must allow students to attend a different and safer school. This law also applies to students who are victims of violent criminal offenses in their public school. When it comes to participating in student clubs, parents have few rights. Under the Equal Access Act of 1984, parents and other community members do not have the right to consistently attend or participate in student clubs. Although student clubs can invite a parent or other community member to be a guest speaker, student clubs must be initiated and run by students. Thus, opponents' charge that students in GSAs are being manipulated by gay activists in the community is unfounded.

¡RECURSOS EN ESPAÑOL!

"Nuestras Hijas y Nuestros Hijos: Preguntas y Respuestas para Padres de Gays, Lesbianas y Bisexuales." Disponible en www.pflag .org/fileadmin/user_upload/NuestrasHijas.pdf

WORKING WITH PARENTS
WHO OPPOSE GSAS

Never underestimate the power of religious fundamentalist parents to organize and oppose any attempt of schools to deal fairly and honestly with homosexuality or transgender issues. They oppose GSAs and any mention of homosexuality. If homosexuality is mentioned, they want it done so only in a negative fashion. Religious fundamentalist parents have imposed their exclusionary agenda on public schools in the states of Alabama, Arizona, Mississippi, South Carolina, and Texas, which prohibit any discussion of homosexuality in schools, or mandate that homosexuality be referred to only in a negative manner (known as *No Promo Homo* laws). In Utah, the State Board of Education prohibits the "advocacy" of homosexuality. These parents have imposed their beliefs on everybody else just to prevent the possibility that schools might send the message, intentionally or unintentionally, that "It's okay to be gay" (Macgillivray, 2004).

Religious fundamentalist parents usually have close ties with national organizations that will assist them in organizing others to inundate school and local government officials with telephone calls, e-mails, and letters protesting the GSA (White, 2006). They will also organize speakers to attend school board meetings and speak against the GSA. Even though they are a minority, they make the most noise and get the most attention. It is at these times, more than any other, when school officials and students need the visible support of parents and community members who support their right to form a GSA.

The Federal Equal Access Act of 1984 gives students the right to form GSAs as long as their district allows other noncurricular clubs. Most districts adhere to the law and allow GSAs. Thus, the parents who oppose GSAs have no legal recourse to prevent them. Because they cannot stop GSAs, they have devised other tactics. For instance, because they believe that GSAs send "pro-gay" messages to students, they argue that the school must give equal time to their point of view that homosexuality is a "condition" that can be overcome, and should invite guest speakers to hold assemblies that promote their antigay beliefs. Another tactic is to encourage other students to start an "Ex-Gay Club" to promote antigay biblical viewpoints. Under the Equal Access Act, students have the same right to form Ex-Gay Clubs as they do to form GSAs. Students also retain First Amendment rights to express their religious views (even antigay religious views) in school, provided they don't do so in a harassing or threatening manner. However, schools do not have to give equal time to all groups or offer assemblies that promote certain groups' beliefs.

Although establishing a GSA can be a stressful and chaotic time, the debate, which the process sometimes generates, can be used as a powerful lesson in democratic process and values. Helping students from the GSA to speak at school board meetings and write letters to the editor teaches them civic participation. Modeling civil discussions between individuals who fundamentally disagree teaches students how to respect others' rights in a pluralistic society. America's public schools are charged with teaching students not only reading, writing, and arithmetic, but also the civic and democratic ideals that will help them to become participating members in the political processes that shape their lives.

SUMMARY

- Don't presume your child has same-sex attractions just because he or she is involved with a GSA. Many students involved in GSAs identify as heterosexual.
- School districts have substantial discretion to set their own policies and curriculum. Under a state's opt-out provisions and because of religious reasons, parents usually have the right to pull their children from educational activities that are part of the mandated curriculum.
- Parents and community members may not regularly attend or participate in meetings of student clubs, including GSAs.
- Parents who support students' right to form GSAs should make their voices heard. Usually, it is the minority of reli-

gious fundamentalist parents who get noticed because they are better organized and protest the loudest.

- Students who start GSAs need the support of parents and caring adults who respect their rights and can help teach them important lessons about democracy and civic participation.

Chapter 7

Conclusion: In Support of Equality and Inclusion

Students have the same right, under federal law, to form a gay-straight alliance (GSA), as they do for any other noncurricular student club. Moreover, students need not directly participate in a GSA to experience the positive effects of having a GSA in their school. Gay, Lesbian, Straight Education Network's National School Climate Survey found that students—whose schools had GSAs—were less likely to report feeling unsafe than students in schools without GSAs (GLSEN, 2003). Pedro M. Garcia-Alonso (2004) studied GSAs for his doctoral dissertation and reports, "GSAs can and do mitigate homophobia and heterosexism in schools to some degree" (p. 190). He gives the following examples:

> Being part of the GSA helped [students] to . . . achieve stronger personal and communal identities . . . They developed a critical consciousness and learned that many of their perceived problems were really society's problems . . . School was perceived to be no longer a place to be avoided, but as a place to confront the heterosexism and homophobia . . .They became empowered, personally and collectively, by working toward a common goal (challenging the system in which they previously believed they could not have an impact). Their impact spread beyond their schools and their communities. (p. 196)

Gay-Straight Alliances: A Handbook for Students, Educators, and Parents
© 2007 by The Haworth Press, Inc. All rights reserved.
doi:10.1300/5921_07

When I was a high school teacher, I was faculty advisor to a group of students who started a GSA (Macgillivray, 2005). The students reported learning valuable lessons about working through layers of bureaucracy, power relationships, compromise, and working with others in a democratic process. One of my students wrote, "I learned more about the adult world than anything I've learned in class." Having worked hard in the face of adversity to establish the school's GSA, two students said, "I felt really proud" and "We made an important difference in bringing issues out of the closet for the sake of tolerance and respect." Another student added, "I've left something for the school to keep." When I asked my students, "Do you feel like student leaders?" one responded for the group, "I think we all do."

Being involved in the GSA helped another of my students remain close to her friends, to whom she had recently come out. She wrote, "I feel a lot better telling my friends who I really am, so I can act like myself and not hide the real me." She recently wrote to me, "The people in the school changed. . . . A lot of people have come out to their friends and schoolmates." Thus, my student's courage and activism paved the way for a more open and democratic school culture.

One of the important lessons that GSAs teach students is about respecting the rights of others who have viewpoints different than their own. The presence of GSAs in America's public schools does not force anyone to accept that "It's okay to be gay." Students with antigay beliefs are free to hold and express them in school, as long as they do so in a manner that is not harassing or threatening. Likewise, students with beliefs that affirm the rights of lesbian, gay, bisexual, and transgender (LGBT) people are free to hold and express them in an appropriate manner. Public education is about the free and open exchange of ideas. GSAs and other student clubs help preserve the democratic exchange of ideas, beliefs, and values that make our country great.

Appendix A

Resources on Sexual Orientation and Gender Identity Development

Healthy Lesbian, Gay, and Bisexual Students Project
This is an online resource from the American Psychological Association, which provides training and resources to school health professionals. Available at www.apa.org/ed/hlgb/homepage.html.

The International Foundation for Gender Education
This Web site contains numerous resources for youth and adults, a bookstore, and opportunities for youth empowerment. Available at www.ifge.org.

Levine, Judith. (2002). *Harmful to Minors: The Perils of Protecting Children from Sex.* **Minneapolis, MN: University of Minnesota Press.**
One of the best books on human sexuality I have ever read. The author cuts through the rhetoric and myths and gives forthright information based on research.

Our Trans Children
This is an online publication of the Transgender Network of Parents, Families, and Friends of Lesbians and Gays (PFLAG). Available at www.youth-guard.org/pflag-tnet/booklet.html.

Gay-Straight Alliances: A Handbook for Students, Educators, and Parents
© 2007 by The Haworth Press, Inc. All rights reserved.
doi:10.1300/5921_08

Savin-Williams, Ritch C. (2005). *The New Gay Teenager.* **Cambridge, MA: Harvard University Press.**
An excellent resource with real case studies, depicting how today's adolescents are rejecting traditionally defined labels like "gay" and "lesbian" and are forging their own unique sexual and gender identities, based on a more fluid and dynamic view of human sexuality.

TransProud
Frequently asked questions about what it means to be transgender. Available at www.transproud.org/faq.html.

Resources on LGBT Issues and Schools

Online

American Civil Liberties Union. *Every Student, Every School: Making Schools Safe for LGBT Youth.* An online resource that offers legal information and training tools for educators and parents to help make schools safer for LGBT students. Available at www.aclu.org/getequal/scho/index.html.

American Psychological Association. *Just the Facts about Sexual Orientation and Youth: A Primer for Principals, Educators, and School Personnel.* Available at www.apa.org/pi/lgbc/facts.pdf.

Gay, Lesbian, Bisexual, and Transgender Issues in Education at www.ianmacgillivray.com.

Gay, Lesbian, Straight Education Network (GLSEN) at www.glsen.org *(recursos en español tambien).*

GSA Network at www.gsanetwork.org *(recursos en español tambien).*

Lambda Legal Defense and Education Fund. *Out, Safe, and Respected: Your Rights at School.* Available at www.lambdalegal.org /cgi-bin/iowa/youthpsa/index.html?page=youth_index *(tambien en español).*

National Center for Lesbian Rights. *Gay-Straight Alliances: Common Legal Questions and Answers.* Available at www.nclrights .org/publications/pubs/gsaqa0703.pdf.

National Gay and Lesbian Task Force. *Issues Affecting Lesbian, Gay, Bisexual, and Transgender Youth.* An online resource that contains statistics on anti-LGBT harassment and policy interventions. Available at www.thetaskforce.org/reports_and_research /education_policy.

Parents, Families, and Friends of Lesbians and Gays (PFLAG) at www.pflag.org.

Videos

Apples and Oranges. (2003). Lynch, T. (Producer), and Fernie, L. (Director). Available from the National Film Board of Canada at www.nfb.ca.

Both of My Moms' Names Are Judy: Children of Lesbians and Gays Speak Out. Available from Lesbian and Gay Parents Association (LGPA) by mail at 260 Tingley Street, San Francisco, CA 94112 or by e-mail at shayndel@aol.com or lgpasf@aol.com.

It's Elementary: Talking About Gay Issues in School. Available from Women's Educational Media online at www.womedia.org/ itselementary.htm *(con subtitulos en español).*

No Dumb Questions. Available online at www.nodumbquestions .com or call 1-800-367-9154.

One of Them. (2000). Torrance, J. (Producer) and Swerhone, E. (Director). Available from the National Film Board of Canada at www.nfb.ca.

Sticks and Stones. (2001). Johnson, G. (Producer) and Padgett, J. (Director). Available from the National Film Board of Canada at www.nfb.ca.

Books and Research

Campos, D. (2005). *Understanding Gay and Lesbian Youth: Lessons for Straight School Teachers, Counselors, and Administrators.* Lanham, MD: Rowman & Littlefield.

Casper, V. and Schultz, S. B. (1999). *Gay Parents, Straight Schools: Building Communication and Trust.* New York: Teachers College Press.

Cianciotto, J. and Cahill, S. (2003). *Education Policy: Issues Affecting Lesbian, Gay, Bisexual, and Transgender Youth.* New York: The National Gay and Lesbian Task Force Policy Institute.

Journal of Gay and Lesbian Issues in Education. Available at www.haworthpress.com/web/JGLED.

Levesque, R. J. R. (2000). *Adolescents, Sex, and the Law: Preparing Adolescents for Responsible Citizenship.* Washington, DC: American Psychological Association.

Lipkin, A. (1999). *Understanding Homosexuality, Changing Schools: A Text for Teachers, Counselors, and Administrators.* Boulder, CO: Westview Press.

Lipkin, A. (2003). *Beyond Diversity Day: A Q & A on Gay and Lesbian Issues in Schools.* Lanham, MD: Rowman & Littlefield.

Macgillivray, I. K. (2004). *Sexual Orientation and School Policy: A Practical Guide for Teachers, Administrators, and Community Activists*. Lanham, MD: Rowman & Littlefield.

Miceli, M. (2005). *Standing Out, Standing Together: The Social and Political Impact of Gay-Straight Alliances*. New York: RoutledgeFalmer.

Wells, K. (2006). *Gay-Straight Student Alliance Handbook: A Comprehensive Resource for Canadian K-12 Teachers, Administrators, and School Counselors*. Ottawa, Ontario: Canadian Teachers' Federation.

Appendix C

1984 Federal Equal Access Act

Title 20 > Chapter 52 > Subchapter VIII > § 4071
§ 4071. Denial of equal access prohibited

(a) Restriction of limited open forum on basis of religious, political, philosophical, or other speech content prohibited
It shall be unlawful for any public secondary school, which receives Federal financial assistance, and which has a limited open forum to deny equal access or a fair opportunity to, or discriminate against, any students who wish to conduct a meeting within that limited open forum on the basis of the religious, political, philosophical, or other content of the speech at such meetings.

(b) "Limited open forum" defined
A public secondary school has a limited open forum whenever such school grants an offering to or opportunity for one or more noncurriculum related student groups to meet on school premises during noninstructional time.

(c) Fair opportunity criteria
Schools shall be deemed to offer a fair opportunity to students who wish to conduct a meeting within its limited open forum if such school uniformly provides that:

Gay-Straight Alliances: A Handbook for Students, Educators, and Parents
© 2007 by The Haworth Press, Inc. All rights reserved.
doi:10.1300/5921_10

1. The meeting is voluntary and student-initiated.
2. There is no sponsorship of the meeting by the school, the government, or its agents or employees.
3. The employees or agents of the school or government are present at religious meetings only in a nonparticipatory capacity.
4. The meeting does not materially and substantially interfere with the orderly conduct of educational activities within the school and
5. The nonschool persons may not direct, conduct, control, or regularly attend activities of student groups.

(d) Construction of subchapter with respect to certain rights
Nothing in this subchapter shall be construed to authorize the United States, or any State, or political subdivision thereof:

1. to influence the form or content of any prayer or other religious activity

2. to require any person to participate in prayer or other religious activity

3. to expend public funds beyond the incidental cost of providing the space for student-initiated meetings

4. to compel any school agent or employee to attend a school meeting if the content of the speech at the meeting is contrary to the beliefs of the agent or employee

5. to sanction meetings that are otherwise unlawful

6. to limit the rights of groups of students which are not of a specified numerical size or

7. to abridge the constitutional rights of any person

(e) Federal financial assistance to schools unaffected
Notwithstanding the availability of any other remedy under the Constitution or the laws of the United States, nothing in this subchapter shall be construed to authorize the United States to deny or withhold Federal financial assistance to any school.

(f) Authority of schools with respect to order, discipline, well-being, and attendance concerns

Nothing in this subchapter shall be construed to limit the authority of the school, its agents, or employees, to maintain order and discipline on school premises, to protect the well-being of students and faculty, and to assure that attendance of students at meetings is voluntary.

Bibliography

Bagby, Dyana. Ga. school's students face new hurdle for gay-straight club: Permission slips required under new state law. *Southern Voice.* August 11. Available at: http://www.southernvoice.com/thelatest/thelatest.cfm ?blog_id=8671.

Board of Education of Westside Community Schools v. Mergens 496 U.S. 226, 271 (1990).

Boyd County High School Gay Straight Alliance v. Board of Education of Boyd County, 258 F. Supp. 2d at 690 (E.D. Ky. 2003).

Boykin, Keith (1996). *One More River to Cross: Black and Gay in America.* New York: Anchor Books.

California Safe Schools Coalition and 4-H Center for Youth Development (2004). Safe place to learn: Consequences of harassment based on actual or perceived sexual orientation and gender non-conformity and steps for making schools safer. Available at: www.casafeschools.org/getfacts. html#research.

Campos, David (2005). *Understanding Gay & Lesbian Youth: Lessons for Straight School Teachers, Counselors, and Administrators.* Lanham, MD: Rowman & Littlefield.

Cianciotto, Jason and Cahill, Sean (2003). *Education Policy: Issues Affecting Lesbian, Gay, Bisexual, and Transgender Youth.* New York: The National Gay and Lesbian Task Force Policy Institute.

Cianciotto, Jason, Cahill, Sean, and Johnson, Dominique (2005). Leaving our children behind: The No Child Left Behind Act of 2001. *Journal of Gay & Lesbian Issues in Education,* 2 (4), 3-21.

Citizens for a Responsible Curriculum v. Montgomery County Public Schools, No. 05-1194 (D. Md. May 5, 2005).

Colín v. Orange Unified School District, 83 F. Supp. 1135, 1140 (C.D. Cal. 2000).

Davis v. Monroe County Board of Education, 526 U.S. 629 (1999).

Doe v. Brockton School Committee, 2000 WL 33342399 (Mass. App. Ct. Nov. 30, 2000).

Gay-Straight Alliances: A Handbook for Students, Educators, and Parents
© 2007 by The Haworth Press, Inc. All rights reserved.
doi:10.1300/5921_11

East High Gay/Straight Alliance v. Salt Lake City Board of Education, 81 F. Supp. 2d 1166, 1197 (D. Utah 1999).

East High PRISM Club v. Seidel, 95 F. Supp. 2d 1239 (D. Utah 2000).

Garcia-Alonso, Pedro M. (2004). From surviving to thriving: an investigation of the utility of support groups designed to address the special needs of sexual minority youth in public high schools. Doctoral dissertation, Loyola University Chicago. UMI Dissertation Abstracts, microform no. 3126026.

Gay-Straight Alliance Network (2007). www.gsanetwork.org

GLSEN (2005). www.glsen.org

GLSEN (2006). Talking About Respect: A+ Messages for Those Working to Create Safe Schools for Lesbian, Gay, Bisexual and Transgender Youth. www.glsen.org/cgi-bin/iowa/all/news/record/960.html.

Griffin, Pat, Lee, Camille, Waugh, Jeffrey, and Beyer, Chad (2004). Describing roles that gay-straight alliances play in schools: From individual support to school change. *Journal of Gay & Lesbian Issues in Education, 1* (3), 7-22.

Hansen v. Ann Arbor Public Schools, No. 02-72802 (E. D. Mich. December 5, 2003).

Haynes, Charles C., Chaltain, Sam, Ferguson, John E. Jr., Hudson, David L. Jr., and Thomas, Oliver (2003). *The First Amendment in Schools.* Alexandria, VA: Association for Supervision and Curriculum Development.

Healy v. James, 408 U. S. 169, 181 (1972).

Henkle v. Gregory, 50 F. Supp 2d 1067 (D. Nev. 2001).

Hsu v. Roslyn Union Free School District No. 3, [85 F.3d 839 (2d Cir. 1996)].

Human Rights Watch (2001). *Hatred in the Hallways: Violence and Discrimination against Lesbian, Gay, Bisexual, and Transgender Students in U.S. Schools.* New York: Human Rights Watch.

ISNA (2005). www.isna.org

Kosciw, Joseph G. (2003). *The 2003 National School Climate Survey.* New York: Gay, Lesbian and Straight Education Network. Available at: http://www.glsen.org/binary=data/GLSEN_ATTACHMENTS/file/300=3.PDF.

Lewin, Tamar (2005). Openly gay student's lawsuit over privacy will proceed. *New York Times.* December 2, p. A21.

Macgillivray, Ian K. (2004). *Sexual Orientation and School Policy: A Practical Guide for Teachers, Administrators, and Community Activists.* Lanham, MD: Rowman and Littlefield.

Macgillivray, Ian K. (2005). Shaping democratic identities and building citizenship skills through student activism: México's first gay-straight alliance. *Journal of Educational Excellence & Equity, 38,* 320-330.

Mayo, Cris. (2004). Queering school communities: Ethical curiosity and gay-straight alliances. *Journal of Gay & Lesbian Issues in Education, 1* (3), 23-36.

McCready, Lance T. (2004). Some challenges facing queer youth programs in urban high schools: Racial segregation and de-normalizing whiteness. *Journal of Gay & Lesbian Issues in Education, 1* (3), 37-51.

Montgomery v. Independent School District No. 709, 109 F. Supp 2d 1081 (D. Minn. 2000).

Nabozny v. Podlesny, 92 F. 3d 446 (7th Cir. 1996).

PFLAG (2005). Nation's schools leave many behind: PFLAG study finds gay students' needs largely ignored. Available at www.pflag.org/ PFLAG_Study_Finds_GLBT_Students_Neglected.302.0.html.

Pope v. East Brunswick Board of Education, [12 F.3d 1244 (3d Cir. 1993)].

Ray v. Antioch Unified School District, 107 F. Supp 2d 1165 (N.D. Cal. 2000).

Sampson, Paula C. (2000). Will participation in a gay/straight alliance mitigate risk behavior in gay and lesbian youth? Unpublished manuscript, Salem State College, Salem, Massachusetts.

Savin-Williams, Ritch C. (2005). *The New Gay Teenager.* Cambridge, MA: Harvard University Press.

Saxe v. State College Area School District, no. 99-4081, slip op. (3rd Cir. February 14, 2001).

Tinker v. Des Moines Independent School District, 393 U.S. 503 (1969).

U.S. Department of Education (1999). Part II: step-by-step guidance: Developing the district's written anti-harassment policy. Available at www. ed.gov/offices/OCR/archives/Harassment/policy1.html.

Wells, Kristopher (2006). *Gay-Straight Student Alliance Handbook: A Comprehensive Resource for Canadian K-12 Teachers, Administrators and School Counselors.* Ottawa, Ontario: Canadian Teachers' Federation.

White, Mel (2006). *Religion Gone Bad: The Hidden Dangers of the Christian Right.* New York: Tarcher/Penguin.

Index

Gay-Straight Alliances: A Handbook for Students, Educators, and Parents
© 2007 by The Haworth Press, Inc. All rights reserved.
doi:10.1300/5921_12

Due Date	Date Returned
FEB 1 4 2009	FEB 1 8 2009
	JUL 2 4 2009

www.library.humber.ca